First-year Composition Guide

2015 Edition

Our Green initiatives include:

Electronic Products
We deliver products in non-paper form whenever possible. This includes pdf downloadables, flash drives, & CDs.

Electronic Samples
We use Xample, a new electronic sampling system. Instructor samples are sent via a personalized web page that links to pdf downloads.

FSC Certified Printers
All of our printers are certified by the Forest Service Council which promotes environmentally and socially responsible management of the world's forests. This program allows consumer groups, individual consumers, and businesses to work together hand-in-hand to promote responsible use of the world's forests as a renewable and sustainable resource.

Recycled Paper
Most of our products are printed on a minimum of 30% post-consumer waste recycled paper.

Support of Green Causes
When we do print, we donate a portion of our revenue to green causes. Listed below are a few of the organizations that have received donations from Fountainhead Press. We welcome your feedback and suggestions for contributions, as we are always searching for worthy initiatives.

Rainforest 2 Reef
Environmental Working Group

Book design by Susan Moore
Cover Design by Ellie Moore

Books may be purchased for educational purposes.

For information, please call or write:

1-800-586-0330
Fountainhead Press
Southlake, TX. 76092

Web site: www.fountainheadpress.com
Email: customerservice@fountainheadpress.com

Eighth Edition

ISBN: 978-1-68036-034-9

Printed in the United States of America

Table of Contents

Introduction to First-year Composition

1

FIRST-YEAR COMPOSITION PROGRAM

Office: 128 Park Hall
Telephone: (706) 542-2128

Administration:

Dr. Christy Desmet, Director
Dr. Deborah Church Miller, Associate Director
Dr. Lisa Bolding, Assistant Director
Mr. Robby Nadler, Assistant Director, UGA Writing Center
Ms. Jane Barroso, Administrative Assistant II

Why Write? FYC and Academic Discourse

Writing is more than simply recording our thoughts, observations, and conclusions. Often, it is a way of discovering what we think or feel. If it were merely the transcribing of what is in our minds, writing would never cause us any problems. Yet how many times have you sat down to write, thinking you knew what you wanted to express, only to find that your thoughts were jumbled or half-formed? Or you may have begun a writing assignment with nothing to say, but found, as you wrote, that you had a range of opinions and information about your subject. In both cases, you discovered what you actually knew or thought only in the act of writing.

Scholars and researchers have long known that writing is itself "a way of knowing." The act of writing improves comprehension of academic material and fixes that material in our memories. This benefit of using writing to master and recall information is discussed further in Robert Leamnson's brief essay, "Learning (Your First Job)," which is included in this *Guide*. Even more important, writing can play a crucial role in the process of learning itself. Writing helps us to make connections among different pieces of information and between information and ideas; it also provides us with a visible record of those connections and (for instance, in the case of multiple drafts) shows us how our ideas change over time. In Leamnson's terms, writing allows us to produce not just "information," but "knowledge."

The kind of writing focused on in First-year Composition (FYC) is called academic discourse. At the University of Georgia, you will be asked to do many different kinds of writing for your classes. As you move into your academic major toward graduation, you will become increasingly involved in writing tasks that draw on specific genres and conventions for your academic field. Psychologists, for instance, engage in different kinds of research and writing than do literary critics. First-year Composition cannot prepare you directly for all these advanced experiences in writing; what we do instead is to give you a grounding in academic discourse, which lays a foundation for later thinking and writing experiences by practicing kinds of writing that seek to inform and persuade a range of audiences. In FYC courses, you will do research on various topics and, together with your teacher and fellow students, work through writing and discussion to use that information to produce knowledge. You will also test the persuasiveness of your knowledge for a variety of audiences, including your teacher, peers, and others.

Two other important goals of FYC are the arts of revision and collaborative critique. For each writing assignment, FYC classes engage in drafting and revision, and for each they engage as well in peer review. You get the opportunity to demonstrate your proficiency in these two crucial areas in the Composing/Revision and Peer Review exhibits in the Electronic Portfolio that you submit as your final requirement in the course. (The Electronic Portfolio is discussed in detail later in this book.) Your skill in these areas will stand you in good stead as you leave your current teacher and classmates, moving through the core curriculum and your chosen major at the University of Georgia. Finally, our program emphasizes writing in the new electronic environments that are important not only to academics and the world of business, but also to individuals in their private lives. You will experience a variety of technologies in FYC, including the program's own electronic writing environment, Emma, which we use both for work during the semester and for constructing final FYC Electronic Portfolios.

The Instructors and Administration of UGA's First-year Composition Program sincerely hope that you enjoy your experiences with writing this year and that you leave our program with the skills and work habits necessary to succeed in writing tasks throughout the curriculum and in the world of work. More broadly, we hope that you leave us feeling confident of your critical thinking, your composing and revision skills, and your ability to comment intelligently on your own and others' writing. Finally, we hope that you will continue to enjoy and practice writing during your years at the University of Georgia. For that reason, we will give you information later about further opportunities for reading and writing at UGA.

Description of First-year Composition Courses

2

All FYC courses share core goals, or learning outcomes, which are detailed below and are also reflected in the program Grading Rubric and capstone Electronic Portfolio assignment (both of which are discussed in greater detail later in this *Guide*).

English 1101: First-year Composition I

English 1101 focuses on informational, analytical, and argumentative writing (the principal genres of academic discourse that students will encounter in many courses across the curriculum) and on research skills and critical thinking. While there are different varieties of English 1101 classes and instructors design their own syllabi, you can get a general sense of what an English 1101 course looks like by consulting the ENGL 1101 Sample Syllabi posted on the First-year Composition Program's website, available online through the English Department Home Page at: http://www.english.uga.edu/.

Prerequisites

Students must either place into English 1101 or pass out of the Academic Enhancement Program.

Goals

In English 1101 students will learn to:

- compose papers in and out of class using processes that include discovering ideas and evidence, organizing that material, and revising, editing, and polishing the finished paper;
- think critically so that they can recognize the difference between opinion and evidence and so that they can support a complex, challenging thesis;
- address papers to a range of audiences;
- understand the collaborative and social aspects of the writing process and demonstrate an ability to critique the writing of themselves and others;
- develop a sense of voice appropriate to the subject, the writer's purpose, the context, and the reader's expectations;

- understand how genres shape reading and writing and produce writing in several genres;
- follow the conventions of standard edited English and MLA documentation;
- use electronic environments for drafting, reviewing, revising, editing, and sharing texts;
- understand and exploit the differences in the rhetorical strategies and in the affordances available for both print and electronic composing processes and texts.

Requirements

Students will create a minimum of three written projects (1,000-1,500 words or longer) that count for at least 50% of the student's final grade. In addition to writing papers and doing other work, all students will create a final electronic portfolio that counts as 30% of their final grade. The ePortfolio is discussed at greater length below.

Course Texts

Hacker et al., eds., *Writer's Help* (web edition)
Text(s) Chosen by Course Instructor
First-year Composition Guide, 2015 ed. (Fountainhead Press)
Any standard college dictionary, such as:

American Heritage Dictionary
Random House College Dictionary
Webster's New Collegiate Dictionary
Webster's New World Dictionary

English 1102: First-year Composition II

Prerequisites

To enroll in English 1102, students must have either exempted English 1101 or passed it with a "D" or better. To graduate, however, students must have earned a grade of "C" in English 1101 and have a combined average grade of "C" in English 1101 and 1102/1103. Students therefore are strongly advised not to enroll in English 1102/1103 until they have received a "C" in English 1101.

According to the University policy on plus-minus grading, a grade of "C-" will not satisfy the requirement for a "C" in ENGL 1101; a combined average of "C-" or 1.7 in English 1101 and 1102 will not satisfy the requirement for a combined average of "C" in the two courses. For more information on plus-minus grading, see: http://www.bulletin.uga.edu/PlusMinusGradingFAQ.html. FAQ #9 is particularly relevant to the requirements of First-year Composition.

Goals

English 1102 shares the core goals, or learning outcomes, of English 1101 but includes as well other goals specific to the course. The content also varies: while English 1101 focuses on different varieties of non-fiction writing, English 1102 focuses on informational, analytical, and argumentative writing through literary texts in various genres; as in English 1101 and English 1103, research and critical thinking skills are also emphasized. While there are different varieties of English 1102 classes and instructors design their own syllabi, you can get a general sense of what an English 1102 course looks like by consulting the ENGL 1102 Sample Syllabi posted on the First-year Composition Program's website, available online through the English Department Home Page at: http://www.english.uga.edu/.

In English 1102 students will learn to:

- read fiction, drama, and poetry and write analytically about them;
- understand literary principles and use basic terms important to critical writing and reading;
- complete written projects in and out of class using processes that include discovering ideas and evidence, organizing that material, and revising, editing, and polishing the finished paper;
- think critically so that they can recognize the difference between opinion and evidence and so that they can support a complex, challenging thesis, and more specifically, document writing using textual evidence;
- address written work to a range of audiences;
- understand the collaborative and social aspects of the writing process and demonstrate an ability to critique the writing of themselves and others;
- develop a sense of voice appropriate to the subject, the writer's purpose, the context, and the reader's expectations;
- understand how genres shape reading and writing and produce writing in several genres;
- follow the conventions of standard edited English and MLA documentation;
- use electronic environments for drafting, reviewing, revising, editing, and sharing texts;
- understand and exploit the differences in the rhetorical strategies and in the affordances available for both print and electronic composing processes and texts.

Requirements

Students will compose a minimum of three written projects (1,000-1,500 words or longer) that count for at least 50% of the student's final grade. In addition to writing papers and doing other work, all students will create a final electronic portfolio that counts as 30% of their final grade. The ePortfolio is discussed at greater length below.

Course Texts

Hacker et al., eds., *Writer's Help* (web edition)
Text(s) Chosen by Course Instructor
First-year Composition Guide, 2015 ed. (Fountainhead Press)
Any standard college dictionary, such as:

American Heritage Dictionary
Random House College Dictionary
Webster's New Collegiate Dictionary
Webster's New World Dictionary

English 1103: Multicultural First-year Composition II

English 1103 focuses on developing effective critical writing, reading, and research skills using core texts that explore the multicultural dimensions of American literature and culture, with an emphasis on African American, Latino/a American, Asian-American, and/or Native American literary traditions. This course offers three hours of credit toward the First-year Composition requirement and satisfies the Franklin College Multicultural Literacy requirement. While English 1103 instructors design their own syllabi, you can get a general sense of what an English 1103 course looks like by consulting the ENGL 1103 Sample Syllabi posted on the First-year Composition Program's website, available online through the English Department Home Page at: http://www.english.uga.edu/.

Goals

In English 1103 students will learn to:

- read fiction, drama, and poetry—with an emphasis on African American, Latino/a American, Asian-American, and/or Native American literary traditions—and write analytically about them;
- situate literature in the historical and cultural context of production and reception;
- understand literary principles and use basic terms important to critical writing and reading;
- compose written work in and out of class using processes that include discovering ideas and evidence, organizing that material, and revising, editing, and polishing the finished project;
- think critically so that they can recognize the difference between opinion and evidence and so that they can support a complex, challenging thesis, and more specifically, document writing using textual evidence;
- address compositions to a range of audiences;
- understand the collaborative and social aspects of the writing process and demonstrate an ability to critique the writing of themselves and others;

- develop a sense of voice appropriate to the subject, the writer's purpose, the context, and the reader's expectations;
- understand how genres shape reading and writing and produce writing in several genres;
- follow the conventions of standard edited English and MLA documentation;
- use electronic environments for drafting, reviewing, revising, editing, and sharing texts;
- understand and exploit the differences in the rhetorical strategies and in the affordances available for both print and electronic composing processes and texts.

Requirements

Students will create a minimum of three written projects (1,000-1,500 words or longer) that count for at least 50% of their final grade. In addition to writing papers and doing other work, all students will create a final electronic portfolio that counts as 30% of their final grade. The ePortfolio is discussed at greater length below.

Course Texts

Hacker et al., eds., *Writer's Help* (web edition)
Text(s) Chosen by Course Instructor
First-year Composition Guide, 2015 ed. (Fountainhead Press)
Any standard college dictionary, such as:

American Heritage Dictionary
Random House College Dictionary
Webster's New Collegiate Dictionary
Webster's New World Dictionary

Alternative Approaches to First-year Composition

The First-year Composition Program is involved in a number of innovative programs on campus and offers several alternative versions of its core courses. Each of these courses has the same prerequisites, goals, and requirements as the more traditional versions.

Honors Courses for First-year Composition II

Honors students have the option of substituting for English 1102 either English 1050H (Composition and Literature) or English 1060H (Composition and Multicultural Literature). These courses have the same general goals as other First-year Composition courses at the University of Georgia, but each class is designed individually by the instructor, often around a special topic.

English Composition for ESOL Students

Special sections of English 1101 and 1102/1103 are reserved for students who have a native language other than American English and who can benefit from an English for Speakers of Other Languages (ESOL) emphasis in these classes. Students enroll only with the permission of the department (POD), but the classes are not marked differently on their transcripts. The ESOL sections, like classes for native speakers, focus on writing academic argument in English 1101 and writing about literature in English 1102/1103. In addition to offering three hours of credit toward the First-year Composition requirement, English 1103 ESOL will also fulfill the Franklin College Multicultural Literacy requirement.

First-year Composition classes for ESOL offer non-native speakers opportunities for vocabulary development, for grammar practice, and for orientation to American styles of writing and organization. Residents of the United States whose first language is not American English, as well as international students, may qualify for these classes. To determine your eligibility and to obtain a POD to register for the ESOL classes, contact the First-year Composition Program Office (706-542-2128) or Jane Barroso at jbarroso@uga.edu.

First-year Composition Synchronous Online

The FYC Program occasionally offers English 1101, 1102, and 1103 sections online throughout the regular academic year. First-year Composition Online has the same goals and requirements as other FYC classes at the University of Georgia: our version of the course has an additional advantage in that it asks students to communicate through writing frequently and in different contexts. These FYC classes are synchronous—that is, students meet virtually in class at designated class times each week.

Special Topics

Experienced instructors may design a special topics version of FYC that is approved in advance by the First-year Composition Committee. These courses often focus on topics related to the instructor's research or scholarly interests, and the sections are marked by a special note in Athena.

UGA Learning Communities

The FYC Program has played a major role in the development of UGA's Learning Communities. As part of each Learning Community, students take a First-year Composition class that is linked to the theme of the Learning Community and sometimes to the content of their other courses in the Community. A description of the UGA Learning Communities and a current list of Learning Communities being offered may be found online at: http://learningcommunities.uga.edu/.

Reacting to the Past

The FYC Program frequently offers sections of composition that incorporate the innovative pedagogy of UGA's Reacting to the Past curriculum. You can find out more about Reacting to the Past at the University of Georgia at: http://www.reacting.uga.edu/.

ENGL 1102E, First-year Composition II, Online, Asynchronous

In the regular, eight-week "Through Term" of summer school, the First-year Composition Program offers English 1102E, a fully online, asynchronous course. Students in 1102E meet all the standard FYC ENGL1102 requirements while completing a series of units (or "modules") as a cohort between specified dates but do not meet as a group during particular class times, either online or face to face.

CHAPTER THREE

Policies and Procedures

3

Placement

Most university students will take English 1101 and 1102/1103 during their first year at UGA. However, some students will receive credit for these courses based on the following tests. Complete information about Placement is available on the Registrar's website, under the heading "Credit from Testing," at: http://www.reg.uga.edu/creditFromTesting.

1. **The Advanced Placement Test**: Students who earn a score of 3 or 4 on the National Advanced Placement Test in Literature and Composition or Language and Composition receive three hours of credit for English 1101; those who earn a score of 5 receive six hours of credit for English 1101 and 1102. All AP equivalencies are available on the Registrar's website: http://www.reg.uga.edu/creditFromTesting/advancedPlacement/uga_ap_credit_equivalencies.

2. **The International Baccalaureate (IB) Test**: Students who earn a score of 4, 5, or 6 on the International Baccalaureate Test at the Higher Level (HL) in English receive three hours of credit for English 1101; those who earn a score of 7 on the International Baccalaureate Test at the Higher Level (HL) receive six hours of credit for English 1101 and 1102. Students who earn a score of 5, 6, or 7 on the Standard Level (SL) test receive three hours of credit for English 1101. All IB equivalencies are available on the Registrar's website: http://www.reg.uga.edu/creditFromTesting/internationalBaccalaureate/uga_ib_credit_equivalencies.

3. **The English Departmental Placement Test**: Students not placed by a national placement test will fall into two groups. Students with an SATV score of 590 and above or an ACT score of 26 or above will place automatically in ENGL 1101 and may register for that class without any further testing; if these students choose to do so, they may take the English Departmental Placement Test voluntarily with an eye to earning three hours of credit for English 1101. Students with an SATV score of 589 or below who have not been placed by a national placement test are **required** to take the English Departmental Placement Test before registering for a First-year Composition class. Specific

information about the Departmental English Placement Test can be found at the Testing Services Website: http://testing.uga.edu/english.php/.

The Departmental English Placement Test consists of two parts, mechanics and rhetoric. A score of 22 (part 1) and 20 (part 2) will place students in English 1102 and gives them three hours of credit for English 1101. Students whose test scores indicate that they might have trouble in English 1101 will write an essay to determine whether they will be advised to take English 1101 or an Academic Enhancement class.

Students should take the test at a First-year Orientation Session. Those who miss the test at Orientation may take it later at University Testing Services in Clark Howell Hall. However, the test is not open to students who have taken or are currently enrolled in First-year Composition here or elsewhere. For more information, please call (706) 542-3183 or visit the website: http://testing.uga.edu.

Absences

Because writing skills develop slowly over time and because in-class activities are crucial to the final Portfolio, students' regular attendance is essential in First-year Composition.

Consequently during fall and spring semesters, on the fifth absence (MWF classes) or the fourth absence (TTh classes), no matter what the reason, students can expect to be administratively withdrawn with a W before the withdrawal deadline and administratively withdrawn with an F after the withdrawal deadline.

For the Summer Thru Term, on the fourth absence, no matter what the reason, students can expect to be administratively withdrawn with a W before the withdrawal deadline and with an F after the withdrawal deadline.

Grade Appeals

It is the instructor's responsibility to judge work and assign grades. Consequently, students with questions about final grades should first discuss those questions with their instructors. If the problem cannot be resolved in discussion, students may prepare a grade appeal in writing according to the guidelines established by the Franklin College Faculty Senate Bylaws, Article V. The bylaws are available at: https://www.franklin.uga.edu/content/faculty-senate-laws. Search for "Grade Appeals."

In First-year Composition appeals, the Director of First-year Composition replaces the Department Head of English in the appeals procedure, in accordance with the English Department bylaws. See Section II, "Appeals at the Department Level." Once a ruling on the grade appeal has been made, if either the student or instructor wants to take the appeal further, the appeal will be conducted according to the guidelines set out in Section III, "Appeals at the College Level."

Before appealing a grade, students should be aware of the following conditions established by the Franklin College Bylaws:

1. A student may appeal a grade if, and only if, he or she is able to demonstrate that the grade was based on factors other than a fair assessment of the student's academic performance in the course.
2. The standards by which grades are assigned, the number and relative weight of assignments on which grades are based, and decisions to allow students to make up or retake missed examinations or assignments, are not grounds for appeal.

Incompletes

The University assigns certain grades that are not computed in the grade point average. The Incomplete ("I") is one of these. It indicates that students have completed almost all of the course work satisfactorily but are unable to meet the full requirements of the course for reasons beyond their control.

When assigning Incompletes, instructors will explain in writing what students must do to finish the course and to calculate a grade, providing a copy of these instructions to both the student and to the FYC office. Students who receive Incompletes may have no longer than three semesters to complete all of their remaining work satisfactorily. Instructors can require that students complete work in a shorter period of time. If an "I" is not removed after three terms (including Summer Thru Term), it changes to an "F." Incompletes are assigned sparingly and at the discretion of the instructor when a small amount of essential work remains. FYC Instructors must first obtain permission from the Director of the First-year Composition Program to assign a grade of "I." An "I" is never assigned prior to mid-semester or for the purpose of allowing students to repeat courses.

General Grading Weights

The meaning of grades is defined generally in the undergraduate version of the *University of Georgia Bulletin*: http://www.bulletin.uga.edu/.

The meaning of grades according to the First-year Composition Program and the Program Grading Rubric is defined as follows:

C	Competent / Credible / Complete	(70-79)
B	Skillful / Persuasive	(80-89)
A	Distinctive	(90-100)
D	Ineffective	(60-69)
F	Extremely Ineffective	(<60)
W	Withdrew	

See the discussion of the FYC Grading Rubric below for more information about grading procedures.

Plus/Minus Grading

Plus and minus grades are assigned only to a student's final average for the course. For the final course grade in First-year Composition, the numerical range for each plus/minus grade is as follows:

A	4.0	(92–100)
A–	3.7	(90–91)
B+	3.3	(88–89)
B	3.0	(82–87)
B–	2.7	(80–81)
C+	2.3	(78–79)
C	2.0	(70–77)
C–	1.7	(68–69)
D	1.0	(60–67)
F	0.0	(<60)

Using Emma in the First-year Composition Program

4

What is Emma?

Emma is a web application designed specifically for writing and revising in academic communities. Students and instructors use Emma throughout the composing process, from brainstorming and drafting through peer review, revision, grading and commenting. Emma organizes tools useful for multi-modal composition within a digital environment. The Emma environment, by providing both public and private spaces where students can collect their work and receive feedback from their peers and instructor, fosters an academic learning community.

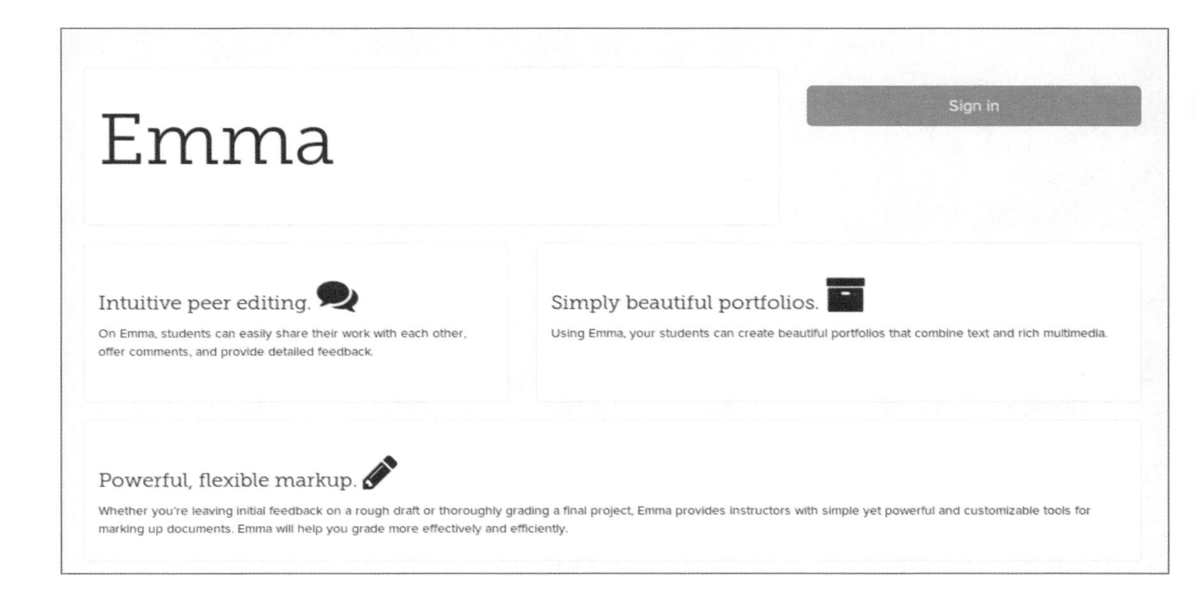

Creating an account

Emma uses UGA's MyID. To create an account, open a web browser to the Emma homepage (http://www.emma.uga.edu) and click the "Sign in" button. Enter your MyID and password. Once you have logged in, please fill out the profile page. Enter your name carefully, as you will not be able to edit it later. You may update your photo and biography at any time.

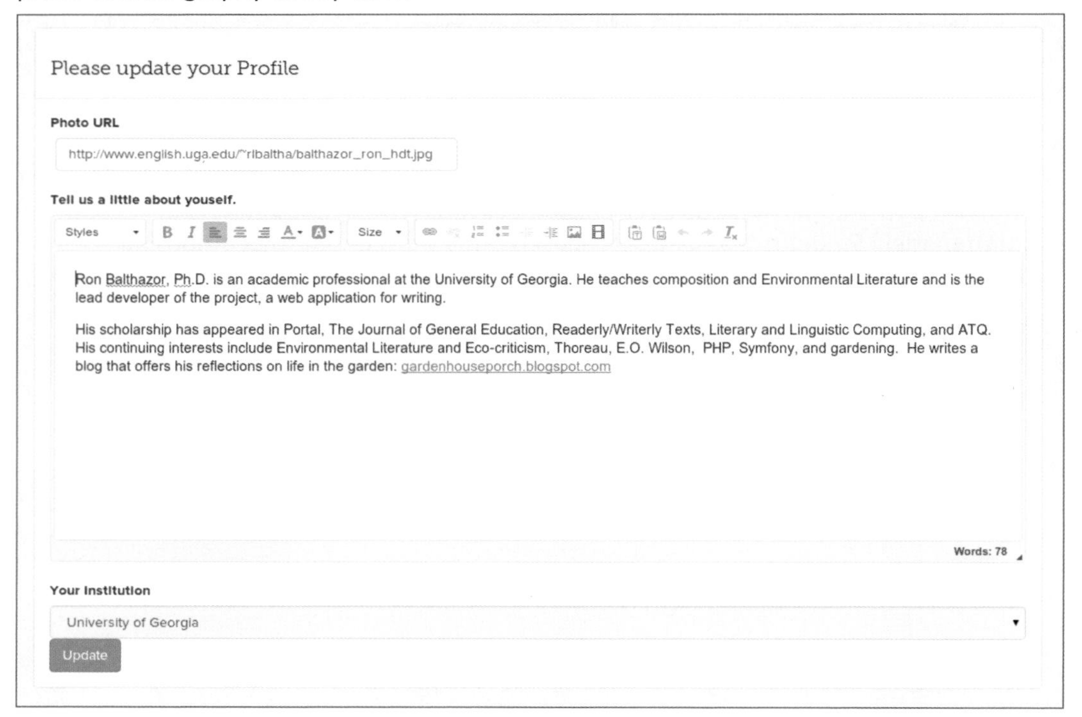

Enrolling in a course

Once you have completed your profile, please enroll in a course. Click the Enroll button and carefully enter your instructor's last name. A list of courses will come up; select your section by clicking the Enroll button (Tip: Note carefully the time of your section—many instructors teach several FYC sections). Until your instructor approves your request, your course will be listed as Pending.

Courses Pending

Demo

Remove

Ron Balthazor , 10:00 am

Please check back soon.

Check now

Once approved, the course will display under Courses Enrolled: click the name of the course to enter it.

Now you are ready to get to work.

The Class Workspace in Emma

Most pages in Emma will have a navigation bar across the top for the major tools in the application and a side navigation bar on the left for working within the current tool. The first page is the Course Home Page, which includes information about the course: the upcoming events in the calendar, an announcement space, and access to the roll and your classmates' profiles.

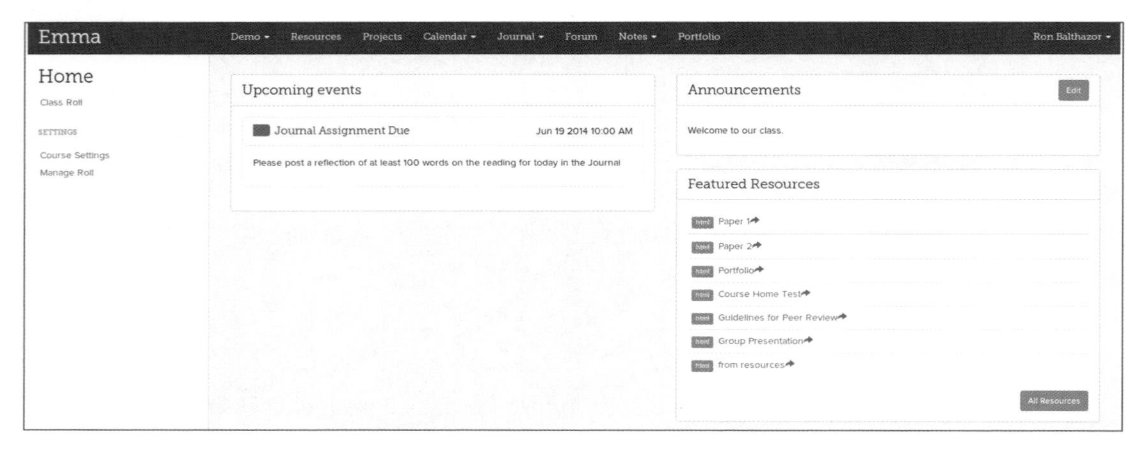

On the top navigation bar, you will see the major tools in Emma. Each will be described below.

Resources

Your instructor will post your syllabus, assignments, readings and other resources here. Note the menu on the left: you will be able to select various categories of files.

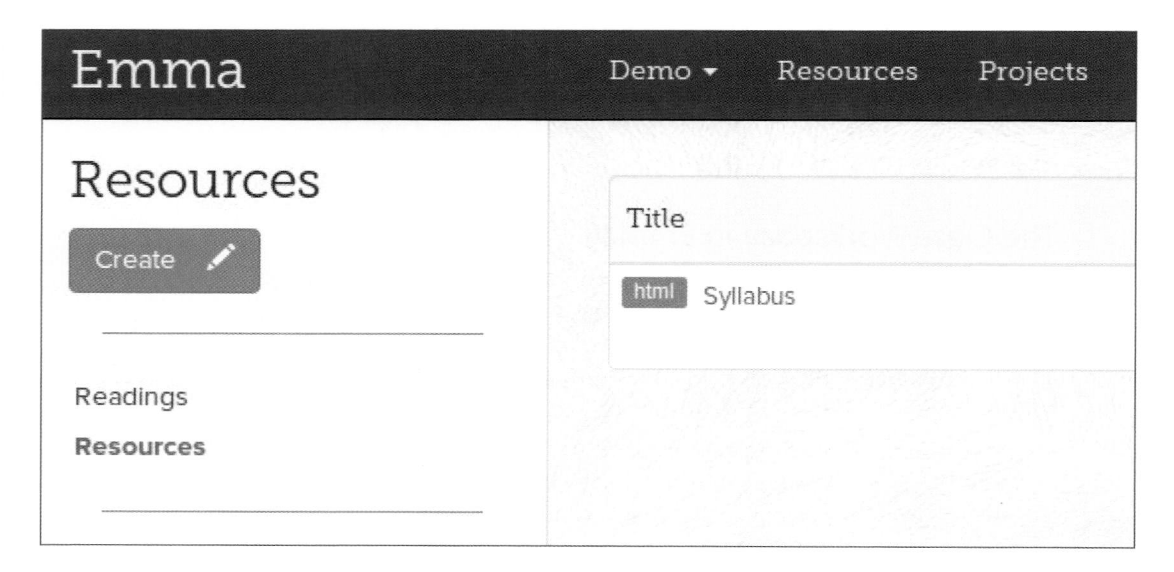

Projects

The Projects space, which is the document-collection space, is where you will do much of your work in Emma. Every document in Emma belongs to a project, and within that project, students add labels to organize their files and drafts. For example, for a Poetry Project, you might have files labeled as Draft 1, Draft 2, Peer Review, and Final. You can find your files and the files of your classmates using the various menus on the left as well as the tool-bar just above the file list.

The First-year Composition Program encourages Process Writing, a practice that emphasizes the stages of composition as much as the final documents. Emma allows you to store and label each stage easily. If you mis-label a document, you can change the label by clicking on the Settings below each file listing.

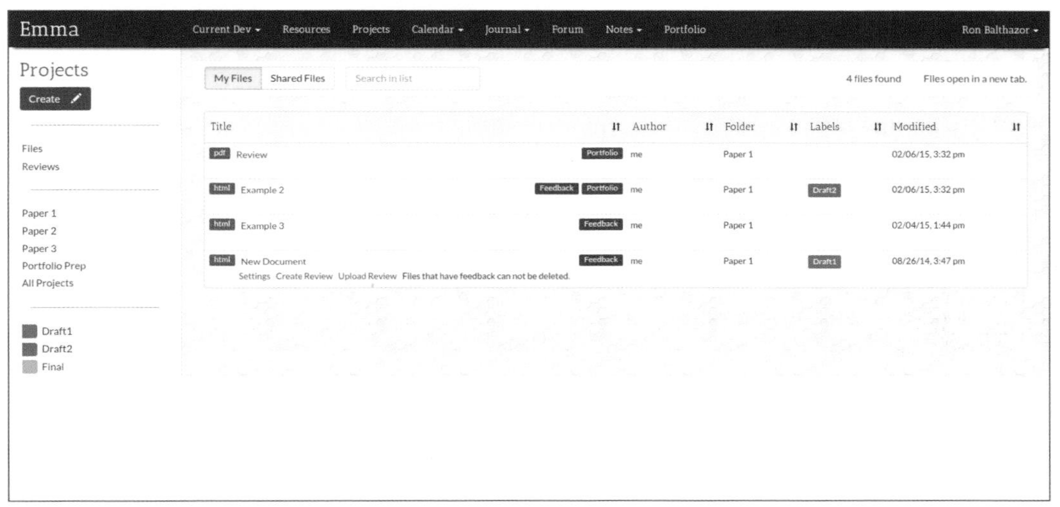

On the left navigation, you will find the Create button (as you will in many of the tools in Emma). Clicking Create gives you a drop-down menu for choosing whether you want to create an Emma document, upload a document or other file, or create a link to other websites or documents.

Similarly, Emma makes it easy to offer Peer Review. Find the document of the peer you would like to review (select Shared Files and then the name of the author on the tool-bar), open it, and then click Create Review.

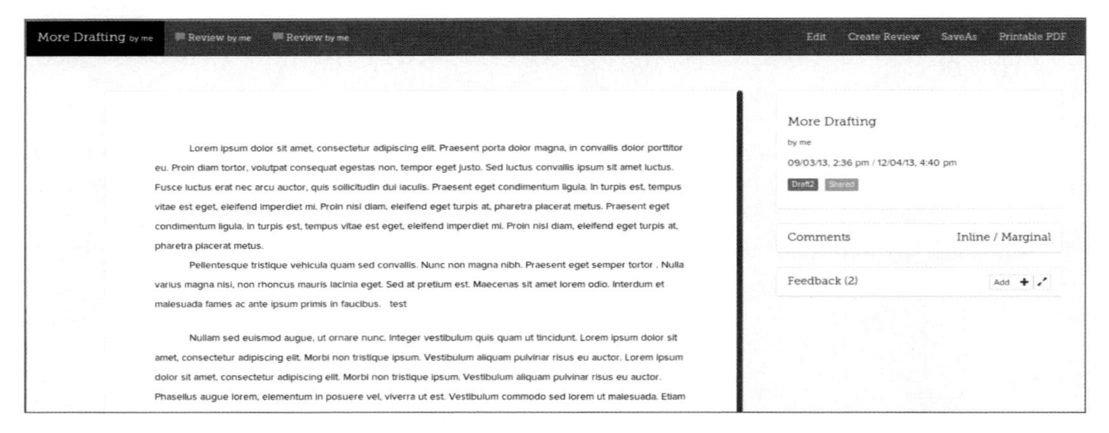

The Peer Review will be connected to the original file and labeled as a Peer Review Document.

Documents created in Emma can take advantage of the application's built-in tools, which include an array of editing and formatting tools, note insertion, and built-in markup highlighting.

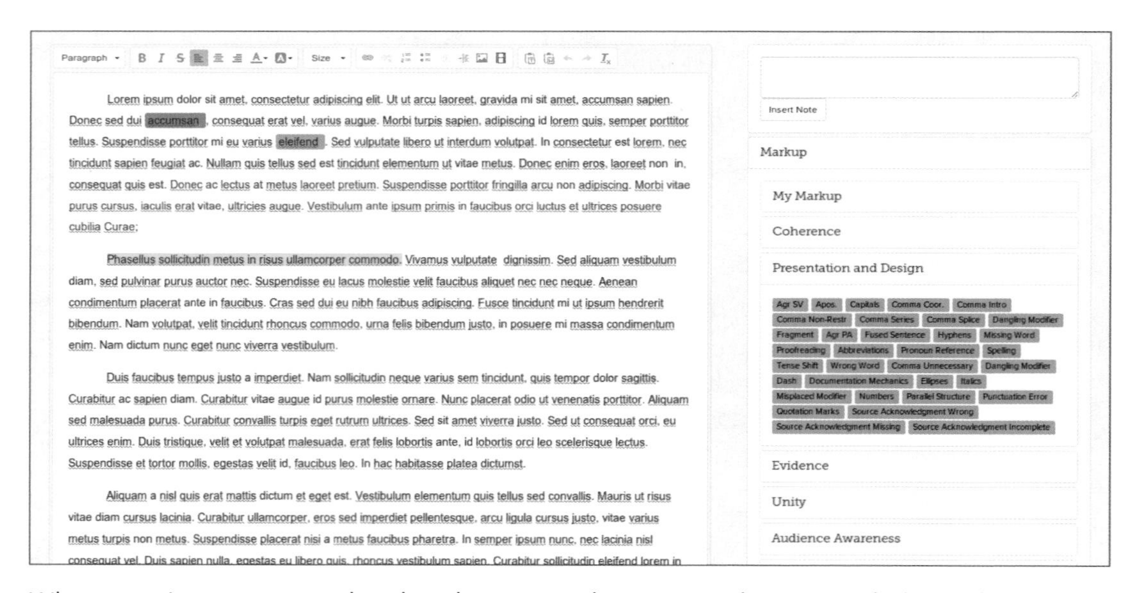

When your instructors read and evaluate your documents, they can include markup links to information and exercises from *Writer's Help* to help you resolve grammatical, mechanical, or rhetorical issues.

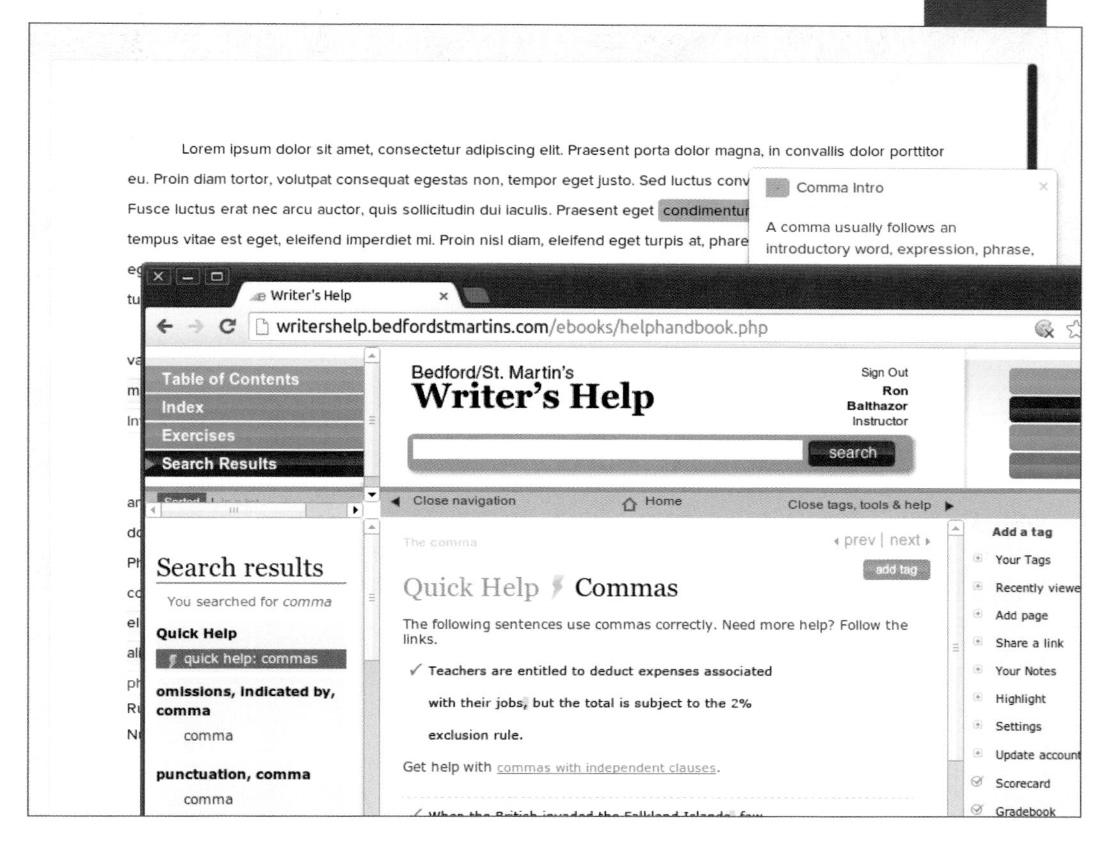

Calendar

Your instructor may post assignments and deadlines in the class Calendar. There are several views, including a month display and an agenda listing that shows events for the whole term. Upcoming events are also displayed on the Course Homepage.

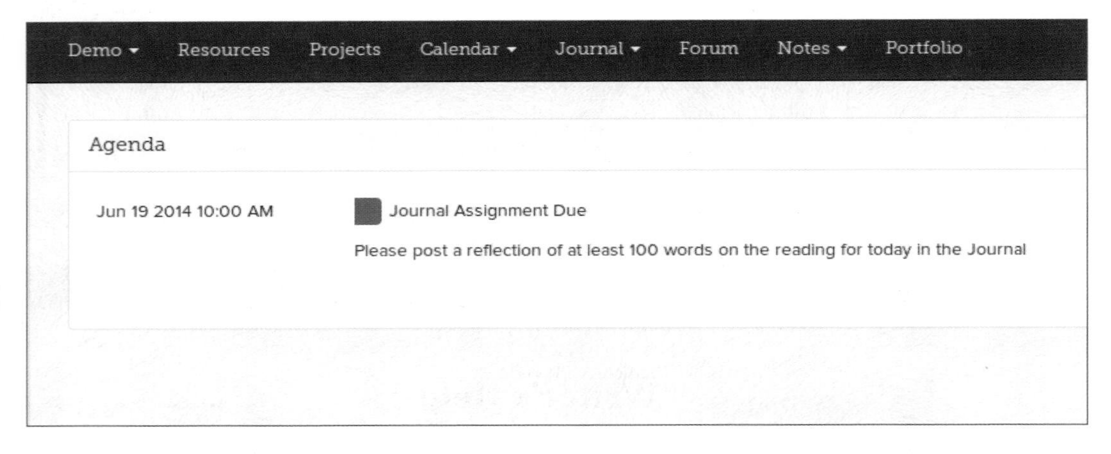

Journal

Emma includes several tools for low-stakes writing. The Journal, as the name suggests, is a simple place for informal writing that is **seen only by you and your instructor**. Click the Create button to get started. Your instructor may offer feedback on your journals; these comments will display beneath your posting.

Forum

The forum offers a shared writing space for conversations. Students can post comments and replies to each other within a discussion topic.

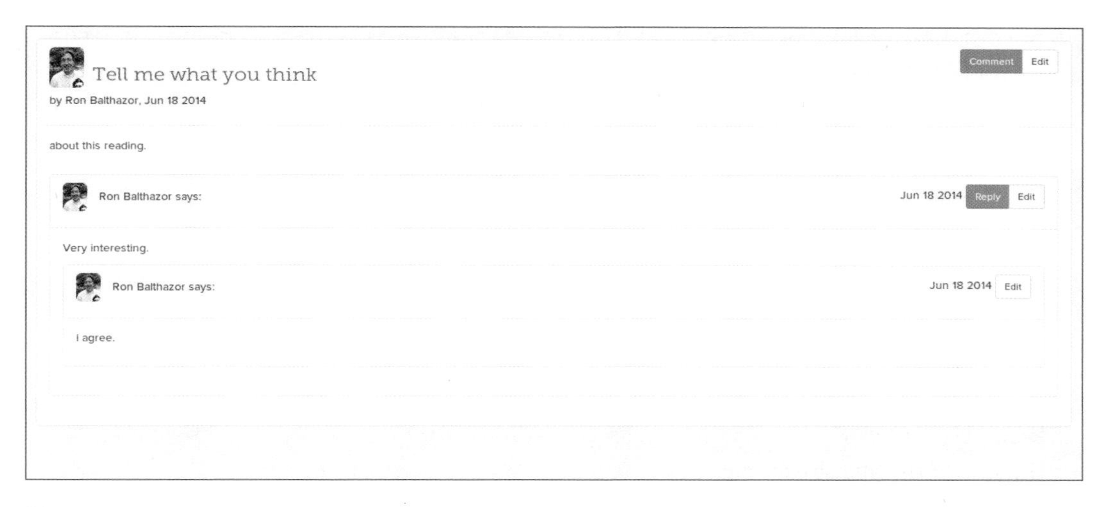

Notes

In the Notes space, you can collect ideas for essays, save research, or take notes in class.

Portfolio

For your final Electronic Portfolio, you will collect and construct exhibits of your work and reflect upon the composition process and other activities in your classroom learning community. To add any previously created and shared Emma file to your portfolio, just click the Add button. (Tip: Emma files **must** be Shared before they can be added to your portfolio).

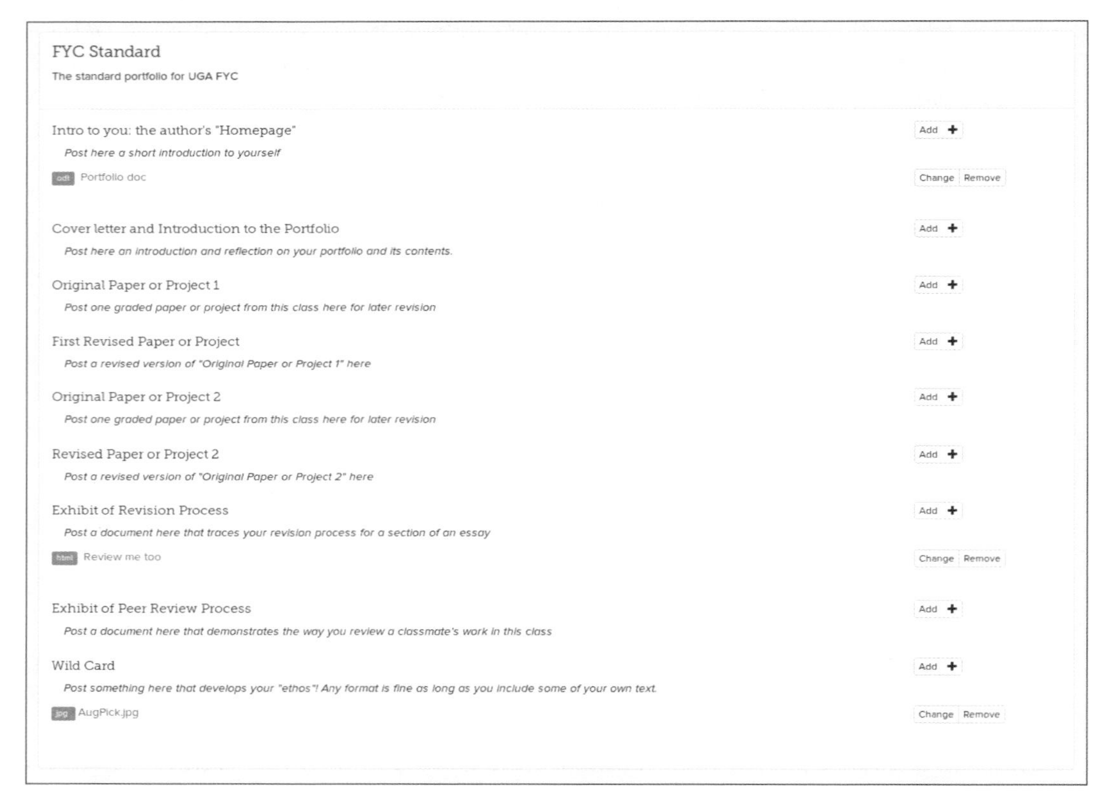

Technical Information

Because FYC at UGA is interested in fostering an open and accessible learning community, Emma uses the ODF standard, which has been adopted by the International Standards Organization (ISO) and the Organization for the Advancement of Structured Information Standards (OASIS). Unlike files saved in proprietary formats—such as .doc, .wpd, or .docx—that can be created and accessed only by using particular word processing software (e.g., Microsoft Word or Pages), .odt files can be created and accessed using a number of free software applications.

In addition, because Emma has been designed as a multi-modal composition platform, it accepts many types of files, as well as ODF files containing multimedia elements such as images and hyperlinks. As long as they do not exceed the 10MB size limit, you can upload and access files in these additional multimedia formats. Depending upon the file format and the browser you are using, these files may be accessed within the browser in Emma, or you may need to download them.

Files in proprietary formats can only be downloaded and accessed using the proprietary software with which they were created; therefore, your instructor may or may not accept assignments in these formats during the course of the semester. **For the final ePortfolio, however, only files in the following formats may be used:** Emma **documents (that is, documents created in the** Emma **editor) and PDF, MP3, or JPEG files**. All these files are generally accessible using Emma-friendly web browsers and standard plug-ins or system software. Microsoft Word documents (.doc or .docx format) will not be accepted in the ePortfolio. (n.b., Firefox, Chrome, and Safari are "Emma-friendly"; Internet Explorer is incompatible with Emma.)

OpenOffice, an open-source word processing application that uses the ODF standard, has been installed on all of the computers in the Emma Lab (Park 117) and the Miller Learning Center (MLC). Students who have personal computers and would like to use them to create documents will need to make sure that they have downloaded and installed a word processor, such as OpenOffice (www.openoffice.org) or LibreOffice (http://www.libreoffice.org), that uses the ODF standard, or they need to ensure that their proprietary word processing software can access and create ODF files. All final drafts created for inclusion in the ePortfolio should be created using Emma documents (eDocs) or should be converted to PDF. Students should always backup their Emma documents with files saved elsewhere in their preferred document format (OpenOffice, Word, etc). Students and Instructors also should remain aware that the file conversion of documents to Emma document HTML files may result in formatting changes, so check final submissions carefully. Students can get help with personal word processing solutions in the main, trouble-shooting Emma Lab, Park 117.

The Emma Lab, where you can bring your Emma questions and problems, is Park 117.

Emma Lab and Support Team

During your time in the FYC program, you might hear your teachers or fellow students mention "the Emma Lab." The "lab," however, actually is housed in three separate rooms: the reservation labs (Park 118 and 119), and the main trouble-shooting lab (Park 117).

If your class is meeting "in the lab" for the day, your teacher has scheduled either Park 118 or 119. These labs contain enough PCs for each student in an FYC class; if you have a laptop and prefer to use it, you are welcome to do so on days that your class is working in the reservation labs. If you are in 119, we encourage you to consider dressing in layers and bringing a jacket. Park Hall is an old building, and 119 is a particularly cold spot. As far as we know, the temperature problem is not, in fact, a haunting.

If you need help with your Emma account or with using Emma in general, though, you'll visit the trouble-shooting lab in Park 117. There, on any week day from 8:05 a.m. to 5 p.m., you will find at least one member of the Emma support team. All members of our support team are experienced teachers who use Emma in their own classrooms, so they are a tremendous resource for students taking FYC courses.

Thanks to a recently-funded grant, Park 117 was renovated during Summer 2015. Policies are posted in each lab and on the "Computer Labs" page of the FYC website (http://www.english.uga.edu)

The most important of these policies is that we do not allow food or drinks. With the addition of new furniture and equipment this year, it is more important than ever to keep these spaces clean and limit their wear and tear. We appreciate your help in preserving the labs for everyone in the FYC program to enjoy.

CHAPTER FIVE

Evaluation of Compositions in the First-year Composition Program

5

What Do Teachers Want?

Because all writing, no matter how personal, attempts to communicate with some audience, writing is a social art. And all writers—whether students writing to develop their skills, amateurs writing to satisfy personal ambition, or professionals writing to support themselves—need to get some reaction to their writing. One form of reaction students get is from **peer review**. By critiquing one another's papers constructively in workshops, student writers gain immediate insight into the effectiveness of their argumentation and prose. Peer review is an important part of the assessment of students' work, for it allows students to get feedback from a range of real readers; the process of responding to other students' essays helps students to become good critics of their own, as well as of others', writing. This skill is important to much college work and is often cited by employers as being crucially important to the world of work. Because peer review is an important skill cultivated in First-year Composition, the capstone Electronic Portfolio includes a demonstration/discussion of the writer's Peer Review process. Students also receive comments and other feedback on some drafts and on graded essays from their First-year Composition teachers; this feedback, along with peer review commentary, is important to the job of revising graded essays for inclusion in the Electronic Portfolio.

Another form of reaction students get to their writing is from their teachers. How teachers grade a written project should interest all students. First, they should understand that no exact correlation exists between the number of marks, or even comments, on a paper and the grade that paper receives. A composition does not begin as a "100" and then lose points as the teacher finds mistakes. Although errors can seriously damage the overall effectiveness of a piece of writing, to write well students must do more than merely rid their work of grammatical and mechanical errors. Effective communication depends primarily on rhetorical concerns; in other words, how effectively does the writing assignment being evaluated meet the needs of a particular audience and accomplish a particular purpose?

To ensure consistency and good communication across the Program, all FYC classes use a common Program Grading Rubric, designed by a volunteer committee of teachers, which explains in greater detail our criteria for different grades. There are four basic categories: Competent/Credible/Complete, which describes compositions that are satisfactory and passing and therefore fall into the "C" range; Skillful/Persuasive, which describes compositions that are well above average—clearly superior to competent work – and fall into the "B" range; Distinctive, which describes compositions that stand out from even very competent work in a singular or important way and therefore fall into the "A" range; Ineffective, which describes work that, for different reasons, does not meet the basic criteria for competency.

Teachers and peers will offer comments and feedback to help you improve your work during successive stages of the drafting process. But when your instructor grades the final draft of your project, she or he will decide, first of all, which of the four categories the composition falls into, using the particular criteria listed under each category for guidance. If your project has Unity, Evidence and Development, and follows basic rules for Presentation and Design, it has earned a C. If in addition, your project also has Coherence and Audience Awareness, you have entered the "B" range, and so forth. Once the instructor has commented on your work and determined the general category into which your work falls, he or she will then decide holistically what place in the given point spectrum your grade falls. For instance, if the project has Unity, Evidence, Presentation/Design, and Coherence, but lacks Coherence, the instructor may determine that it falls toward the lower end of the Skillful/Persuasive spectrum (80-89 points): in such a case, your composition might earn an 82 or 83. If your project has, in addition to the qualities detailed above, a strong personal voice that clearly demonstrates Audience Awareness through its ability to communicate with "real people," it might earn an 87 or 88.

Of course, there is no exact mathematical formula for determining grades. For instance, it is always possible that a project that contains a few grammatical errors (Presentation/Design) or changes direction at one point (Unity) excels so clearly in more advanced criteria—say, a sense of voice showing a clear Audience Awareness or excellent transitions from one idea to the next supporting Coherence—that the instructor decides it really should earn a B. In general, though, students should expect to satisfy all of the criteria for the Competent/Credible/Complete category in order to receive a passing grade.

The FYC Grading Rubric gives both students and teachers a common vocabulary for talking about writing quality and a set of important criteria for evaluating projects and/or compositions that are submitted for a grade during the semester and also those revised works submitted in the capstone electronic portfolio. Some instructors use a special template in Emma that links comments not only to criteria of the FYC Grading Rubric (which helps students to understand their grades), but also to sections of *Writer's Help* relevant to each criterion (which helps students to improve their writing). Students can also use the Rubric to assess the progress of their own work as they move through the drafting process. Finally, as the Rubric indicates, teachers may include special requirements that affect students' final grades, adding or subtracting points based on those special, stated requirements. If you excel in these extra requirements or fail to meet them, your grade may be raised or lowered accordingly.

What Grades on Compositions Mean

In more specific numerical terms, the meaning of grades is defined by the undergraduate version of the University of Georgia Bulletin: http://www.bulletin.uga.edu. The meaning of grades according to the First-year Composition Program is defined as follows:

C	Competent / Credible / Complete	(70-79)
B	Skillful / Persuasive	(80-89)
A	Distinctive	(90-100)
D	Ineffective	(60-69)
F	Extremely Ineffective	(<60)
W	Withdrew	
I	Incomplete	

Plus / Minus Grading

Plus and minus grades are assigned only to a student's final average for the course. For the final course grade, the numerical range for each plus/minus grade is as follows:

A	4.0	(92-100)
A-	3.7	(90-91)
B+	3.3	(88-89)
B	3.0	(82-87)
B-	2.7	(80-81)
C+	2.3	(78-79)
C	2.0	(70-77)
C-	1.7	(68-69)
D	1.0	(60-67)
F	0.0	(<60)

FYC Grading Rubric

Here is the actual rubric that your teacher will use when evaluating your essays and often will encourage you to use when critiquing your peers' essays and making judgments about your own work.

Student's Name______________________________________ **Teacher** ________________________________

Project #____ **Special Assignment Requirements:** ____

Conference____________

"Enter a pertinent quote here." (Teachers can self-select)

Writing Center__________

_____ Competent/Credible/Complete

If you meet these first three standards, you are writing competently and you will earn a grade of "C." (70-79)

1. **Unity**
   - Contains a center of gravity, a unifying and controlling purpose, a thesis or claim, which is maintained throughout the composition.
   - Organizes writing around a thesis or according to the organizational requirements of the particular assignment (e.g., summary, narrative, argument, analysis, description, etc.).
2. **Evidence/Development**
   - Develops appropriate, logical, and relevant supporting detail and/or evidence.
   - Includes more specific, concrete evidence (or details) than opinion or abstract, general commentary.
3. **Presentation and Design**
   - Follows WH guidelines for Standard English grammar, punctuation, usage, and documentation.
   - Meets your teacher's (or the MLA's) and the First-year Composition program's requirements for length and/or format.

_____ Skillful/Persuasive

If you meet all of the competency standards above and, in addition, achieve coherence and exhibit audience awareness, you are writing skillfully and you will earn a grade of "B." (80-89)

4. **Coherence**
   - Uses words and sentences, rhythm and phrasing, variations and transitions, concreteness and specificity to *reveal and emphasize the relationship* between evidence and thesis.
   - Explains how, why, or in what way the evidence/detail provided supports the claim/ point /thesis/topic ideas.
   - Incorporates evidence from outside sources smoothly, appropriately, and responsibly.
5. **Audience Awareness**
   - Demonstrates a sense that the writer knows what s/he's doing and is addressing real people.
   - Reflects a respect for values that influence ethos (e.g., common ground, trustworthiness, careful research).

_____ Distinctive

If you meet all of the competency standards, achieve coherence and exhibit audience awareness, and, in addition, demonstrate a mastery of one or more features of superior writing, you are writing distinctively and you will earn a grade of "A." (90-100)

6. **Distinction**
   - Your writing stands out because of one or more of the following characteristics: complexity, originality, seamless coherence, extraordinary control, sophistication in thought, recognizable voice, compelling purpose, imagination, insight, thoroughness, and/or depth.

Essay Grade ______ **+/- Points for special assignment requirements** ______ = **Final Grade**

_____ Ineffective

If your work does not meet competency standards, either because you have minor problems in all three competence areas (1-3 above) or major problems in one or two competence areas, you will earn a grade of "D" (60-69) or "F" (<60), and you should schedule a conference with your teacher.

University of Georgia First-year Composition Grading Rubric 2015-2016 5/19/2015

Using the First-year Composition Grading Rubric's Vocabulary

We use the FYC Grading Rubric throughout our First-year Composition program because it helps teachers, tutors, students, and sometimes advisors, parents, and administrators to understand what our program values and looks for in student writing. Many teachers use an electronic version of this Rubric and mark compositions with coded electronic tags and inserted comments, while other teachers clip or staple a paper copy of the Rubric, along with their handwritten notes, directly to student work. Whether paper or electronic—whichever form of the Rubric they use—teachers depend on the standard Rubric's language to guide their evaluation of student compositions, while students must depend to some degree on the Rubric's language to understand their teachers' comments. Finally, the Rubric's common vocabulary helps students comment on one another's work and to make judgments about their own projects. The Rubric helps to keep all parties on the same page!

In order to help students (and teachers) use the Rubric most effectively, here we discuss some of the key terms:

Competent/Credible/Complete

In order to receive a passing and satisfactory grade of "C," students' work needs to meet the three principal criteria of Unity, Evidence/Development, and Presentation and Design.

1. Unity = Staying on topic and providing structure

"Contains a center of gravity, a unifying and controlling purpose, a thesis or claim, which is maintained throughout the composition."

First-year compositions can be organized in many different ways. Compositions may have an implicit or explicit thesis, or they may simply have a unifying purpose or theme. In any unified composition, however, every sentence and every word will contribute in some way towards the exposition and development of the "main" idea.

Notice, too, that at the level of Competency "unity" does not require a particularly complex, clever, or imaginative thesis, nor does unity require strong coherence. Typically, a thesis can be described as having two parts: a topic plus a comment about that topic. For example, if my thesis were "cats are annoying," then the topic would be "cats" and the comment would be "are annoying." In a composition with such a thesis, unity only requires that every sentence be related to either the topic ("cats") and/or the comment on that topic ("are annoying"). Teachers and peer reviewers sometimes need to read between the lines to notice an underlying or implied unity. For instance, sometimes a writer includes an apparently unrelated comment, such as "Cats often have long, fluffy fur." The writer may need to add just a word or two (perhaps adding a word or two about annoying shedding, allergies, or long cat hair on couches!) to firmly demonstrate unity.

"Organizes writing around a thesis or according to the organizational requirements of the particular assignment (e.g., summary, narrative, argument, analysis, description, etc.)."

Simply put, to "organize writing around a thesis" or other central point means that the composition reveals, under examination, an overall organizational plan or strategy. To evaluate organization, a reader might ask questions such as these: Could this work be outlined? Does each paragraph play a role in developing the thesis? Does the work have a definite beginning, middle, and end? An organized composition might use logical, spatial, chronological, or even associational order—but the strategy will be employed to suit the topic and the purpose of the writing project.

2. Evidence/Development = Providing support (examples, details, or specifics)

"Develops appropriate, logical, and relevant supporting detail and/or evidence."

This criterion asks you to note whether the writer uses examples and/or other evidence to support his/her argument, position, or idea and whether that evidence is fairly used, accurate, and relevant.

Depending on the type of writing assignment, good evidence may include anecdotes, images, descriptions, dialogue, quotations (from primary and/or secondary sources), graphs, and/or charts; typically, evidence will include quotations from a variety of sources—often including the texts read in class. In this case, you are evaluating the quality of evidence and sources used. To evaluate the **quality** of evidence, a reader might ask questions such as these: Did the writer use examples accurately and not take them out of context? Were selected quotations clearly related to the writer's argument? Was the source of the evidence credible? Or for a descriptive or narrative assignment, readers might ask if a particular scene is described with accurate, concrete, and specific details.

"Includes more specific, concrete evidence (quotations, interviews, charts, statistics, details, description, observation, and dialogue) than opinion or abstract, general commentary."

This criterion asks you to gauge **quantity** of evidence. To evaluate the quantity of evidence, you might ask questions such as these: Has the writer made many general claims about a topic without supplying specific supporting evidence? What is the ratio of sentences providing opinions compared to sentences providing support (giving examples, quotations, and details)? Typically, readers hope to find a good deal more evidence than opinion. On the other hand, you might ask: Does the writer string together a long series of quotations and facts into lists or lengthy quoted passages? Is there too much unincorporated and unexplained evidence?

3. Presentation and Design = Correctness and formatting issues

"Follows guidelines for standard English grammar, punctuation, usage, and documentation."

To meet this criterion, here is a general rule of thumb: To pass at the level of Competency, a paper should contain two or fewer major errors plus four or fewer minor errors per 250-words (about a page). If there are no major errors, a composition should have eight or fewer minor errors per 250-words. All the major errors have to do with either sentence boundary recognition or Standard English grammar issues. For our purposes, the major errors are:

- Comma Splice
- Fragment
- Fused Sentence
- Subject/Verb Agreement
- Pronoun/Antecedent Agreement

All other errors are considered minor errors. If a student's paper has more errors than the standard described above, the paper is not meeting competency guidelines for a final draft.

Remember, however, that this standard is just a guideline. Simply lacking a large number of errors does not necessarily make a project "Competent" or passing. As we point out in the Introduction to this section: "A composition does not begin as a '100' and then lose points as the teacher finds mistakes."

"Meets your teacher's (or the MLA's) and the First-year Composition Program's requirements for length and/or format."

The standard format and documentation requirements for First-year Composition follow those for MLA formatting. Teachers, however, may have special requirements, which might include the use of specialized or alternative style sheets (such as CBE, CSE, APA, or Chicago), images, graphs, video, particular fonts, minimum word counts, bibliographies, appendices, notes, abstracts, etc.

EXAMPLES:

Here are two brief examples from the 2015 Barnett Award winners that effectively demonstrate the qualities needed in a Competent/Credible/Complete composition. Each essay shows how **evidence** can be used effectively to support different purposes. In addition, both excerpts reveal careful attention to **presentation and design** (the samples are error free and follow standard documentation and formatting requirements). Finally, even in these brief excerpts, each writer's overall purpose and topic is clear, meeting the standard for **unity**.

In the first example (below), we see ENGL1102 writer, Brian West, develop a **clear central thesis**, contributing to a unified academic argument (UNITY). He argues that the two poems, Lucille Clifton's, "forgiving my father" and Theodore Roethke's "My Papa's Waltz," share not only similar themes, but also stylistic strategies. In addition, West develops substantial EVIDENCE in the body of his essay as he deftly integrates **paraphrase, summary, and direct quotations** from each of the poems to support his thesis. In the first example below, West introduces his thesis (in bold). In the second selection (the paper's fifth paragraph), Wests incorporates both paraphrases and direct quotes. Finally, West fulfills the third area of competence, PRESENTATION & DESIGN, by providing accurate, thorough documentation and formatting and editing his paper to MLA standards. (Examples of evidence are highlighted in red; the thesis and topics are in purple.)

Paragraph 1

Damaged relationships, especially those between close family members, are often never repaired. Unfortunately, this damage commonly leads to a situation in which one is left alone to reconcile after the other has passed. Those who have experienced this situation know the difficulty of accepting and forgiving. **Lucille Clifton, in her poem "forgiving my father," and Theodore Roethke, in his poem "My Papa's Waltz," explore their own turbulent relationships with their fathers. Both poets comment on the painful nature of these relationships and use writing as a means of reconciliation.** The two styles, which include a resentful confrontation and an ambiguous narrative, show the versatility of this process.

Paragraph 5

As we read closer, we find that Clifton uses a similar strategy, as she hints at possible conflicted emotion. While her language is harsh and her attitude toward her father is bitter, she hints that this may not be her sole sentiment. Immediately following a comment about her feeling of being owed, she presents a statement which appears to counter her demands of reconciliation. She admits to her father that "you were the son of a needy father, / the father of a needy son" (12 -13). She goes on to concede that "you gave her all you had / which was nothing. You have already given her / all you had" (14-16). These words, especially when read aloud in the reserved, anguished tone that the lower case style proposes, plainly reveal Clifton's alternate emotions. Within these lines, she admits to a justification that she may need if she is to truly forgive her father. Similarly, Roethke uses diction to indicate his willingness to accept his father's flaws by identifying positive aspects of their relationship. He does this primarily by alluding to the father's role as a caretaker. He mentions his father's "palm caked hard by dirt" (14). When considering that the father's work entailed tending to a large greenhouse, the reader surmises that this is not a disapproving remark about the father's hygiene, but rather an admiration of his exhausting labor. Through this remark, Roethke, like Clifton, deftly and skillfully presents himself with justification for his father's behavior. Here, the reader begins to see the hints of forgiveness and the implication of reconciliation.

Excerpted from: "Dealing with Damaged Relationships"
ENGL 1102
Student: Brian West
Teacher: Rafaella Wilson

Unlike the primary text quoted in West's literary analysis above, ENGL1101 writer Scott Davis, in his researched composition "Fine, whatever . . . " deploys direct observation, images, expert testimony, and a range of sources to provide EVIDENCE validating his argument that the use of emoticons and emoji in Computer Mediated Composition (CMC) effectively contribute to the human ability to communicate shades of meaning and are, in a way, simply an extension or evolution of traditional punctuation. Below is paragraph four of his composition in which he quotes and paraphrases expert sources and draws on common experiences to provide evidence for the continuing evolution of punctuation now occurring in digital spaces.

Paragraph 4

In text messaging the characteristics of brevity, speed, and simplicity are the name of the game, and with this purpose much punctuation is often dropped, leading to many punctuation marks acquiring new meanings. The primary and most important example is the period. The line break has replaced the period as a separator of speech, and the period has slowly shifted to accept a new meaning (Crair 2). Additionally, "The unpunctuated, un-ended sentence is incredibly addicting," says Choire Sicha, editor of the Awl. "I feel liberated to make statements without that emphasis, and like I'm continuing the conversation, even when I'm definitely not" (qtd.in Crair 2). In text messaging and even in IM messages, the default way to end your phrase is to just end it, no period involved. I mean, why would we use a period when everything we are typing is usually one sentence and is just meant to represent conversation? Thus, since the appearance of a period is rare in the texting world, it adds new meaning when it *is* used because the reader tries to figure out why it was used. The period is not used as a punctuation mark anymore but rather as a tone differential, subliminal message, or indication of the end of the conversation (not just the sentence) (Crair 3). That tone differential has come to have a negative connotation, usually either to indicate that the writer is upset, angry, or another similar emotion. Ben Crair explains that "people use the period not simply to conclude a sentence, but to announce 'I am not happy about the sentence I just concluded'" (1). It is truly an amazing innovation, in that a punctuation mark that was used to express separation and pause in speaking and literature has now adapted to indicate tone (Crair 3).

Davis's composition also presents an excellent sample of distinctive "Presentation and Design" because his incorporation of images goes "above and beyond" correct mechanics and grammar, providing not only pathetic appeal, but in addition, presenting logical evidence for and clarification of his claims. Below is a screenshot of Davis's page three, showing his distinctive use of images.

Davis 3

< Messages Katy Details

Hey, don't forget about work tomorrow 6:30 0:)

ER, 6:15 at least

Breakfast available on request

Sounds good - breakfast would be great :)

Your ham and cheese egg burrito is hot and ready

characteristics of normal human conversation, such as audio tone and visual cues, had been lost (Sherwood 1). In fact, statistically, 93% of human communication occurs visually through body language, and through tone of voice (Harmon 70). This is where the emoticon comes in. Judith Meyer says, "Nowadays, we often use writing as a form of quick communication in text messages and chats. These don't leave the time to carefully consider how we can avoid misunderstandings of our tone, so emoticons are a very useful tool" (et al 2). With the help of the emoticon, we are able to clarify emotional context with what would have been otherwise ambiguous emotional standing within a message, as well as make text messaging more human. Take, for example, the text message displayed above on the left, from a friend of mine to me.

She started the conversation with, "Hey, don't forget about work tomorrow 6:30 0:)", reminding me to give her a ride to work. However, if she had said the same phrase without the smiley face featuring a halo, the message could have come across as selfish, nagging, and possibly even condescending. With the addition of a simple smiley face, especially an angelic reference of

Excerpted from "Fine, Whatever. . . "
ENGL 1101
Student: Scott Davis
Teacher: Al Dixon

Skillful/Persuasive

In order to reach the level of a "Skillful/Persuasive" paper, an argument must have two additional qualities: Coherence and Audience Awareness.

4. Coherence = The "Flow"

"Uses words and sentences, rhythm and phrasing, variations and transitions, concreteness and specificity to reveal and emphasize the relationship between evidence and thesis."

In general, while students can achieve unity by creating a strong thesis and staying on topic, they create coherence by focusing their reader's attention on the relationship between thesis and evidence (or theme and detail). Creating Coherence is about controlling emphasis.

Students may use diction to emphasize the thesis-to-evidence connection by choosing words carefully, by repeating key words and phrases, by avoiding the repetition of unimportant words and phrases, and by using transitional phrases accurately. Writers can also use syntax – that is, sentence structure – to direct emphasis by varying sentence structures, by employing syntactical effects such as parallelism and antithesis, or simply by changing sentence length or reversing normal Subject-Verb-Object sentence patterns. In evaluating coherence, you may ask these questions: Has the writer used syntax and diction to create links and bridge gaps between his or her thoughts? Does the writer use transitional phrases and words frequently and accurately to help the reader follow the writer's thinking from sentence to sentence and from paragraph to paragraph? Does the writer's use of repetition, parallelism, figures of speech, and rhythm help to emphasize main points, or does the writer's choice of diction and syntax distract the reader from the main ideas?

"Explains how, why, or in what way the evidence/detail supports a point/claim/thesis/topic ideas."

Writers need to include explanations. In fact, writers usually need to explain why each detail or item of support has been included in an essay. It is a rare bit of evidence that is so clear that it speaks for itself. Coherence develops as writers explain how each part of their arguments' evidence provides support for their theses.

"Incorporates evidence from outside sources smoothly, appropriately, and responsibly."

The writer will consistently incorporate quotations and references to other outside sources into her own sentences. Coherent writers move often between paraphrasing, summarizing, and brief selected quotations from different sources. Few, if any, quotations will be left "hanging"—that is, standing alone in separate sentences; instead, they will be embedded in the writer's own sentences, usually with explanatory remarks linking the quotations to the topic or thesis. Lengthy quotations, serial quotations, or long summaries rarely occur in a "Skillful" writer's composition. The excerpt below offers good examples of smoothly inserted quotations and responsible citation practices.

EXAMPLE:

In the example below, 2014, ENGL1103 Barnett Award writer Sarah Landry develops a subtle thesis that explores the role of gender in creating the emotional power of Alanis Morissette's song, "You Oughta Know." In this excerpt, Landry moves skillfully among expert opinions and her own reading of Morissette's lyrics, summarizing, paraphrasing, and quoting, yet never losing sight of her own position and purpose. Notice how Landry uses explanatory sentences, key words, linking phrases, repetition, parallel structures, and transitional phrases to create COHERENCE, keeping the reader focused on Landry's own argument—that Morissette's song is "a lyrical lesson in female empowerment." (Examples of increased coherence are highlighted in **Green.**)

Power From Pain

Word for bleeding word, Alanis Morissette's 1995 hit single "You Oughta Know" is, well, a lot more than just a hit single. The lyrics, coupled with the heavily symbolic music video, prove to be a journey through outrage, suffering, and envy, and Morissette has a peculiar way of following her written path. Instead of shying away from her agony, she embraces it, allowing her edgy, uncut voice to stagger through each injustice until she has overcome her struggle. Overall, the song is an angst-filled roller coaster of emotion that the listener and the artist must endure together. But how does one endure this? What is it, specifically, that Alanis Morissette seems to be drawing her harsh resilience from? The answer is gender roles. As Morissette sorts through the emotional wreckage of her failed relationship, she challenges and manipulates the strengths and weaknesses associated with both genders in order to establish herself as a strong, honest woman.

Coming from an album that *Words & Music* describes as a "fearless set of songs on which she [Morissette] empties herself of pain," the duality of emotion in "You Oughta Know" is hardly surprising. Just as it makes up the core of the song's meaning and intent, it will also make up a good deal of this analysis. First, every aspect of Morissette's vocal and physical performance alerts listeners that she is feeling aggressive and angry and that she doesn't plan to remain silent about it. A certain sadness defines the performance too, and if one watches carefully, it also structures her actions in the video.

Although Morissette prefaces "You Oughta Know" with the soft, unassuming declaration that she "wishes the best" for her past lover and his new lover, she quickly dives into the rage that carries the entire song (Morissette). The listener finds herself peppered with accusatory questions and statements that Morissette's growling voice only enhances. "Did you forget about me, Mr. Duplicity?" she seems to demand, each syllable in the word "duplicity" emphasized like an individual punch (Morissette). And as she reels across the video's makeshift "stage," swaying and thrashing and allowing her hair to fall over her face in an untamed mass, one can only assume that she is feeding the same fire that rests behind the lyrics. By venting her aggression in this way, Morissette is ultimately drawing from an emotion that is typically associated with males, therefore challenging what is expected of her in terms of gender. The purpose, however, comes across in the fact that she appears bold and unafraid. She doesn't care that she isn't behaving like a calm, "decent" woman, but is remaining true to what she feels.

Believe it or not, the underlying sadness in Morissette's performance does not contradict her aggression. It actually builds on her strength. The artist herself told *W & M* that this song (along with many others on the album *Jagged Little Pill*) gave her the "opportunity to not only be honest with myself, but in some cases, with the people I was upset with." So, with brutal honesty and a complex twist on an otherwise pathetic emotion, the vocalist wails through the chorus, stating, "It's not fair, to deny me / Of the cross I bear that you gave to me." In the music video, her face curls inward as if she is crying, and during later repetitions, she even "crumbles" or falls to her side with an equally pained expression (Morissette). Admittedly, sadness (especially when shown openly) is considered a weakness of the female gender, but Morissette toys with her agony, and as the listener becomes aware that she is unashamed by this display of emotion, they see her as a strong, independent, and perhaps outspoken woman.

Excerpted from "Power from Pain"
ENGL 1103, 2014
Student: Sarah Landry
Teacher: Miriam Brown-Spiers

5. Audience Awareness = Writing should speak to real readers

"Demonstrates a sense that the writer knows what s/he's doing and is addressing real people."

Showing that a writer "knows what s/he's doing" means that the writer works to develop his or her credibility (ethos). He or she might mention and/or demonstrate particular knowledge or research concerning a topic, demonstrate comfort and familiarity with appropriate jargon or professional vocabularies, or simply use sound logic and clear reasoning in his or her discussion. Credibility can be, however, developed in many ways.

"Reflects a respect for values that influence ethos (e.g., common ground, trustworthiness, careful research)."

Respect for an audience and values can be shown at every level. A reader evaluating writing for respect might ask these questions: Has the writer chosen an appropriate level of formality in his or her diction—avoiding the too formal for an audience of close friends, the too familiar with teachers or general audiences? Has the writer avoided unnecessary jargon or slang? Has the writer avoided sexist or racist language? Is the writer's choice of supporting examples and evidence appropriate, fairly used, relevant, and judiciously applied? Does the writer show a high level of integrity about facts and correctness at every level? Does the writer implicitly and explicitly show courtesy and good will towards readers whose opinions may differ? Does the writer acknowledge counter-arguments and other positions?

EXAMPLES:

Three very different excerpts from the 2015 Barnett and Moran Award winners demonstrate the qualities of "respect for values" and "a sense that the writer knows what h/she's doing."

In the first example, notice how this excerpt from Scott Davis's paper, "Fine, Whatever. . . ," combines an overtly colloquial voice—addressing the reader as "you," posing rhetorical questions, using first person pronouns, and explaining or providing examples – with effectively integrated expert evidence and personal observation. This combination creates a sense of both personality and authority. While Davis's voice is personal, it is also convincing and well-informed.

In the second example, Brian West's traditional scholarly literary analysis, "Dealing with Damaged Relationships," West directs his analysis to a general, formal academic audience. West adopts the conventions and impersonal style of academic discourse. He avoids the first-person singular, carefully integrates quotations into his own sentences, adopts formal diction, and documents sources fully in the text and Works Cited, following the proper disciplinary (MLA) style.

In the final example, an excerpt from the biography exhibit of Alyssa Shrewsbury's ENGL1101 final portfolio, we hear the appropriately informal and personal voice of a young woman sharing her own life experience to an audience of classmates and teachers. Her repeated use of first-person pronouns (I, me, myself) along with specific descriptions of her personal experiences as "evidence" seem well-suited to the occasion. To be aware of your audience is to know which conventions to adopt and follow in each new writing venture.

(Examples of adaptations to show AUDIENCE AWARENESS are highlighted in orange.)

Selection 1: Scott Davis

In the digital age, expressing your emotion can be as easy as typing one or two punctuation characters, such as a colon and parentheses to make a smiley face :). You have probably seen this string of characters or other ones like it various times throughout texting, email, IM messaging, or other examples of CMC (computer-mediated communication), but where did it all come from? CMC is essentially any human communication that occurs by two or more electronic devices ("Computer-mediated communication"), which would inherently include texting. The character shown above, as well as :(:-) :-(:P :/ and many others, are examples of "letters" or "configurations" in the alphabet of emoticons. However, perhaps the "emoji," easily considered emoticon 2.0, is of more importance and weight in today's communications, as it is more modern: ☺☹. Although you, the reader, may not be as familiar with these as you are with emoticons, you have still likely seen them by some form of CMC. While most people over the age of 25 likely think of emoticons and emojis as pointless and as adding little meaning to writing (Marsden 2), these characters have a big effect on today's CMC, especially emotionally. In fact, they were made explicitly for emotional expression, created to fill the emotional, tonal, and modal hole that had been created naturally in CMC. Additionally, long before the emoticon, ever since writing was established, we have had punctuation as a writing tool to help establish tone and emotion. In a world of short and brief text messages, punctuation and emojis/emoticons determine the tone of the text message more than the actual words do. This makes the textual interaction more human and allows us to communicate more naturally as well as personally by allowing us to add visual components of communication that were originally lost.

Excerpted from "Fine, Whatever . . ."
ENGL 1101
Student: Scott Davis
Teacher: Al Dixon

Selection 2: Brian West

The diction Clifton uses demands a response; she shows clearly the pain her father caused her. She uses the metaphor of financial debt to reveal her feelings of being owed, calling on her father to make a payment that is overdue. **She calls to her father to reconcile; "today is payday, payday old man" (line 5).** She yearns to collect the repayment of the emotional deficit that she was left with. She also uses this metaphor to show how she eventually concedes to her father's passing. **She uses an eerie metaphor for her father's coffin, commenting on "debtor's boxes," which "no accounting will open them up" (22-23).** With this metaphor, Clifton reveals that she accepts that her father has moved on, even if the debt has not been collected. Though she is left to endure the anguish left by her father, lamenting over his passing only causes more agony.

Conclusion and Works Cited

In essence, "forgiving my father" is a personal exploration of resentment with undertones of forgiveness and compassion, while "My Papa's Waltz" is an affectionate narrative with conflicted feelings of animosity and regret. Each poem has a unique delivery, but neither appears to be distinctly less effective than the other in its purpose. Both poets eventually reach a resolution that is at least productive, if not satisfying. To these poets, it seems that merely talking about their problems is enough to elicit improvement. The authors prove to the reader that this type of cognitive process is worth the pain that it sometimes entails. Though it is often difficult, relationships can be mended, as Roethke and Clifton demonstrate, if one makes a substantial and impartial attempt at forgiveness.

Works Cited

Clifton , Lucille. "forgiving my father." *Making Literature Matter: An Anthology for Readers and Writers*. Ed. John Schilb and John Clifford. Boston: Bedford/St. Martins, 2012. 270-71. Print.

Roethke, Theodore. "My Papa's Waltz." *Making Literature Matter: An Anthology for Readers and Writers*. Ed. John Schilb and John Clifford. Boston: Bedford/St. Martins, 2012. 273. Print.

Excerpted from: "Dealing with Damaged Relationships"
ENGL 1102
Student: Brian West
Teacher: Rafaella Wilson

Selection 3: Alyssa Shrewsbury

Living By a New Title

Art has always been my hobby, but for me, viewing myself as an artist was intimidating and required me to change my perception of who an artist could be. I had it built up in my mind that only one kind of person could be an artist and because I did not fit the stereotypical portrayal of a moody, recluse hipster carrying around a mug of herbal tea at all times, who was I to pretend that I was an artist? This disconnect between who I am and what I do not only restricted my ability to create, but also obscured my perception of who I could be. It was not until two summers ago when I visited the High Museum of Art that I was able to take on the title of an artist.

During my visit, the featured artist was Johannes Vermeer. He is best known for the Masterpiece, "The Girl With the Pearl Earring." With such a famous and mysterious work on display, I did not expect a quiet self-portrait by Rembrandt to engage and inspire me the most that day. The plaque by Rembrandt's self-portrait described how he was perceived in his day. Rembrandt was known for being fun and outgoing. He was, simply put, a lover of life. Thinking about the words on the plaque, I realized something that I was never able to admit it to **myself** before: I felt unworthy to be called an artist.

Excerpted from Final Portfolio Bio
ENGL 1101
Student: Alyssa Shrewsbury
Teacher: Paula Rawlins

Distinctive

To earn the highly coveted grade of "A," a writer must go beyond basic criteria required for a competent composition, exceed the expectations for a skillful composition, and provide something else that gives the composition real "value added," sticks in the reader's memory, or catches her attention.

6. Distinction: A few words about distinction

"Your writing stands out because of one or more of the following characteristics: complexity, originality, seamless coherence, extraordinary control, sophistication in thought, recognizable voice, compelling purpose, imagination, insight, thoroughness, and/or depth."

No single quality reveals distinction; that's why we've listed so many possibilities. A paper should **meet standards in all five of the other criteria** before it is considered for "Distinction." This does not mean that students' papers must necessarily excel in all five criteria (although many will and most will excel in three or more criteria), but papers should be average or better in every category and should not be deficient in any category when being considered for Distinction.

The FYC Grading Rubric was designed by a volunteer team of instructors who carefully examined a range of compositions, deciding what qualities papers at different grade levels share in common. Based on their work, we now have a common vocabulary that students and teachers can use to understand how to succeed in First-year Composition.

Electronic Portfolios in the First-year Composition Program

6

The First-year Composition Electronic Portfolio

Every student who takes a First-year Composition course at the University of Georgia composes an electronic portfolio over the course of the semester. The ePortfolio gives students an opportunity to revise and polish their work—even after it has been evaluated for a grade during the semester—to showcase their work in a personalized context, to reflect on their writing and their writing processes, and, finally, to "publish" their work to a broader audience. The use of an electronic portfolio for all FYC classes means that students have an opportunity to raise their grades through steady work and revision; but it also means that students need to schedule adequate time to do their very best work in the portfolio, as it counts for 30% of their final grade.

Students develop portfolios throughout the semester using the First-year Composition Program's Emma writing environment—adding, updating, and revising elements under teachers' directions and using the support available in the Emma Lab in Park Hall 117. Students will also find that using feedback from their classmates in peer review sessions, both in and out of class, will make portfolio development a much more rewarding process.

The details of using Emma to compose your ePortfolio will be described during Emma Orientation sessions and during classes. In addition, individual teachers will make specific assignments for various parts of the portfolio. In broad outline, however, the essential seven components of our ePortfolios are consistent in every FYC course and are described briefly below:

> **Note:** *You cannot re-use or recycle any exhibit from your English 1101 portfolio, including the Biography or Introductory Reflective Essay, for your English 1102/1103 portfolio. This would be Academic Dishonesty and handled under the Academic Honesty policy and procedures.*

Elements of the Portfolio

Front Page: Biography

The Biography is a short introduction to you, the author of the portfolio. Your class or teacher may specify particular information to include in your Biography, but, in general, the Biography should act as an author's headnote.

Images on your Biography page are optional, but readers like them, so you should try to include some image that is relevant. You can select a representative image (a windmill, a horse, or anything you can find on the Web—just remember to include a citation), or you can select an image of yourself. Think of it as a dust jacket image on the back of a book—how do you want to represent yourself? The goal of your Biography page should be to establish a credible ethos.

Note: The Biography MUST be constructed as an Emma *eDocument in order to display properly in your* Emma *portfolio. We strongly recommend creating it using eDocs. You must also check carefully to make sure that the Biography displays properly, as this will provide portfolio readers with their first impression of you as a writer.*

Introductory Reflective Essay (IRE)

The most important element in your ePortfolio, the Introductory Reflective Essay provides a reader with an introduction and guide to the rest of your work. A strong IRE ties together all the exhibits in your portfolio; it helps you describe and reflect on your writing processes, with your exhibits providing the supporting evidence. The Reflective Introduction is also the first item evaluators will read after they open your Biography page. Your teacher may provide you with a specific prompt or s/he may direct you to some specific portion of the FYC program sample prompt to help you get started. In your IRE, you might discuss how the various exhibits you have chosen for your portfolio reveal the way you have engaged with the goals of the course listed earlier in this *FYC Guide* and/or the FYC Grading Rubric's criteria. Some very successful portfolios have re-organized the author's work for the semester around a common theme that the writer sees in her or his own work. 750-1500 words is the average length for an IRE, although some of the Moran Award winners have written longer IRE's.

Two Revised Compositions from the Course

You will include in your Electronic Portfolio two of the three graded papers you have written for the class, revised and polished and posted to the portfolio. They should be substantive and well-argued, carefully edited, error free, and completely, thoroughly, and correctly documented in MLA format.

> *Note about the Revised Compositions: We recommend a thorough revision for the Revised Compositions exhibits in your Portfolio—not just a quick proofreading for surface errors. Could more evidence be developed, a new perspective raised, for instance, a change in tone attempted, or a firmer line of reasoning followed?*

When choosing compositions to put in your Electronic Portfolio, think about how they will work together to help make the portfolio a unified whole. Some students choose the compositions that received the highest grades, but this is only one criterion. You may want to choose the compositions you like the best, the ones you can improve the most, or the ones that fit best with your chosen theme.

Exhibit of Composing/Revision Process

This exhibit demonstrates your composing and revision process. Typically, students construct this document by copying and pasting the same or similar sections of a selected composition into a single document. You can then add commentary explaining the significance of the different versions, pointing out and explaining the changes you made through successive drafts. The Revision Exhibit gives you a chance to demonstrate not so much your best products for the semester, but the skill set that you have built up over the course of the semester. The trick is to make it easy for a reader to follow the process; the explanation is just as important as, or perhaps more important than, your chosen examples. This exhibit gives you a chance to reflect on your progress throughout the semester and to perform a self-assessment.

Exhibit of Peer Review Process

One of the goals for all FYC courses states that students will "demonstrate an ability to critique the writing of themselves and others." For this exhibit, which speaks directly to that goal, you will select and post to your portfolio one of the peer reviews that you have written during the semester, including commentary to help the reader understand your peer review process. One option is to choose a review you completed for one of your classmate's papers. Try to choose one that you believe was helpful and focused; you might want to ask your classmates about which ones were helpful to them. You may also copy and paste together several brief examples of peer reviews you have completed and construct a new document with inserted commentary. Explanations about the assigned peer review are often helpful here, too. As in the previous case, the Peer Review Exhibit gives you a chance to demonstrate not so much your best products for the semester, but the skill set that you have built up over the course of the semester. As with the Composing/Revision Process Exhibit, the Peer Review Exhibit gives you a chance to reflect on your progress throughout the semester and to perform a self-assessment.

Wild Card

This exhibit is up to you. The only limitations are that your Wild Card 1) must be an electronic file or link that "fits" in your Emma portfolio; and 2) must include some of *your* writing, which may appear as captions, short descriptions, or introductory commentary. In the past, students have submitted journals, papers, photos with captions, short stories, poems, letters, song lyrics, scans of drawings with comments, news articles, podcasts, and music files. Some students create new exhibits especially to fit with their portfolio theme. In thinking about selecting or creating a Wild Card, consider how it fits into your overall portfolio rationale and how its inclusion will impact ethos and pathos.

Special Note on Presentation and Publication of your ePortfolio

Importance: The electronic portfolio, as the capstone project that showcases your achievements and learning, is very important; it counts for 30% of your final grade.

Digital Publication: The ePortfolio is not merely a loose collection of word-processed documents, but a unified digital artifact whose parts fit together in a rational and harmonious manner. It is therefore not enough to just put your final documents in the Portfolio Prep folder. You must construct the ePortfolio using the Portfolio Tool; this is the only way that your readers can access your work. If you do not complete the ePortfolio properly, you may receive a grade of zero for this important project.

Presentation and Design: Just as the Grading Rubric considers Presentation and Document Design as important to the rhetorical success of your essays, so too does the ePortfolio. Your portfolio therefore must meet the highest standards for presentation and document design; failure to do so will seriously hurt your grade for the ePortfolio.

Readability and Access: Finally, this is an electronic (rather than a print) portfolio that will be read online by two different readers. It is your responsibility to make sure that:

- the front page of your ePort and all of the exhibits display properly without significant formatting issues;
- all exhibits are in one of the acceptable file formats (see below);
- can be navigated easily and efficiently by your readers.

Open your portfolio on several different computers and click through all the exhibits to make sure that the portfolio is reader-friendly.

How Are FYC ePortfolios Evaluated?

At the end of the semester, every FYC student's Emma Portfolio is read by at least two FYC teachers: his or her own teacher and one other. The presence of a second reader gives writers another real reader for their work. If the scores assigned to any portfolio differ by ten or more points, a third FYC teacher also reads and scores that Portfolio. To arrive at a final portfolio score, the two closest scores awarded are averaged. The Portfolio grade counts as 30% of an FYC student's final course grade. (See your teacher's syllabus for more information.)

Technical Note: Acceptable File Formats for ePortfolio Exhibits

Because at least two teachers must be able to read successfully your ePortfolio online and not all teachers will have available the proprietary word processing package contained on your personal computer, the FYC Program accepts only the following file formats for ePortfolio Exhibits that are primarily text documents:

- PDF
- Emma eDocuments

Emma eDocuments: This accepted format is easy to use; eDocs have the added advantage of allowing you to do all your writing and editing in the web browser itself.

PDF documents: Students who include a large number of images in their documents or have special design and formatting needs often choose to upload the documents in their portfolios as PDF documents. This is the only format in which you can be absolutely sure that the document appears exactly the same in your word processor and the web display.

In order to evaluate them, teachers read portfolios holistically. This means that the readers "norm" themselves, getting a sense of what "constitutes" an A, B, C, etc. among the group of portfolios that they are reading, then judge each portfolio as a whole, assigning it a single grade. As teachers read through students' portfolios, they particularly gauge how well a student's Introductory Reflective Essay (IRE) describes the content found in the other exhibits and whether or not the student has been able to use writing to express his or her own encounter with goals and evaluative criteria of the course. In other words, expect FYC teachers to use the IRE as a guide for reading your other documents, in order to get a sense of how well they match the expectations you set up in your Introduction. Of course, teachers always look for evidence of care, originality, hard work, and excellent writing, but in the portfolio we are also interested in students' ability to write reflectively and accurately about their own writing.

In addition, teachers often use the Rubric below, based on the standard FYC rubric and using the same or similar terminology, to help them get started when they are beginning to evaluate portfolios each semester. They may also point you towards this rubric to help you evaluate your own or your classmates' portfolio during a workshop.

ELECTRONIC PORTFOLIO RUBRIC

BIOGRAPHY

- Is present and complete;
- Is carefully proofread and edited, with very few errors of a grammatical, mechanical, or typographic nature.
  [CCC] ______________________________

- Shows clear and appropriate awareness of audience;
- Gives a coherent picture of the writer.
  [SP] ___________________________

- Is distinctive for its:
  - imaginative quality;
  - extraordinary and effective care in craftsmanship and presentation;
  - prose style;
  - compelling authorial voice;
  - persuasive argumentation.

  [DIST]___________________________________

INTRODUCTORY REFLECTIVE ESSAY

- Is present and complete;
- Makes a clear and complete statement about the writer's ethos, development, and/or skill set that is more than an autobiographical narrative or list of exhibits (unity-thesis);
- Offers a clear rationale for the choice of exhibits and their order (unity-organization);
- Explains the role of each exhibit in the overall portfolio and in proving the thesis (evidence);
- Is carefully proofread and edited, with very few errors of a grammatical, mechanical, or typographic nature.
  [CCC] ____

- Offers a strong, and vivid understanding of the writer and writing (audience awareness);
- Is particularly persuasive about how exhibits contribute to the whole portfolio (coherence).
  [SP] ____

- Is distinctive for its:
  - imaginative quality;
  - extraordinary and effective care in craftsmanship and presentation;
  - prose style;

- compelling authorial voice;
- persuasive argumentation.

[DIST] ____________________

TWO REVISED MAJOR COMPOSITIONS

- Are present and complete;
- At a minimum, meet the FYC Rubric qualifications for CCC;
- Are carefully proofread and edited, with very few errors of a grammatical, mechanical, or typographic nature.

[CCC] ____________________

- At a minimum, meet the FYC Rubric qualifications for SP.

[SP] ____________________

- At a minimum, meet the FYC Rubric qualifications for a DIST or a "high" SP that shows extraordinary thoughtfulness and care.

[DIST] ____________________

EXHIBIT OF COMPOSING AND/OR REVISION PROCESS

- Present and complete;
- Offers a clear and complete statement about and/or example of the composing and/or revision process (unity);
- Supports that thesis with specific examples (evidence);
- Presents the examples in a logical manner (unity-organization);
- Is carefully written, edited, and proofread, with essentially no distracting errors of a grammatical, mechanical, or typographic nature.

[CCC] ____________________

- Offers strong and vivid examples of the writer and writing (audience awareness);
- Is particularly persuasive about how the examples support the thesis (coherence).

[SP] ____________________

- Is distinctive for its:
  - imaginative quality;
  - extraordinary and effective care in craftsmanship and presentation;
  - prose style;
  - compelling authorial voice;
  - persuasive argumentation.

[DIST] ____________________

EXHIBIT OF PEER REVIEW PROCESS

- Is present and complete;
- Offers a clear exhibit of a peer review (unity);
- Arranges one or more examples of peer review in a logical manner (unity-organization);
- Is carefully presented so that both the original and comments are easily seen. Errors in grammar or spelling don't interfere with conveying comments (presentation & design).

  [CCC] ____

- Shows a strong, and vivid understanding of the writer and commentary (audience awareness);
- Is persuasive because comments show a clear understanding and response to the work (coherence).

  [SP] ____

- Is distinctive for its:
  - imaginative quality;
  - extraordinary and effective care in craftsmanship and presentation;
  - prose style;
  - compelling authorial voice;
  - persuasive argumentation.

  [DIST] ____

WILD CARD

- Is present and complete;
- Fits into the portfolio as a whole in a logical way that is described in the introductory reflective essay;
- Is carefully written, edited, and proofread, with few errors of a grammatical, mechanical, or typographic nature that distract from the purpose of the exhibit.

  [CCC] ____

- Offers a strong and vivid understanding of the writer and writing (audience awareness).

  [SP] ____

- Is distinctive for its:
  - imaginative quality;
  - extraordinary and effective care in craftsmanship and presentation;
  - prose style;
  - compelling authorial voice;
  - persuasive argumentation.

  [DIST] ____

CHAPTER SEVEN

Academic Honesty and Plagiarism

7

UGA Academic Honesty Policy

The University of Georgia is committed to "A Culture of Honesty." The First-year Composition Program supports this commitment and follows strictly the university's policies and procedures for dealing with possible instances of academic dishonesty. Information about "A Culture of Honesty" and the "UGA Academic Honesty Policy" and procedures can be found at the web site of the Office of the Vice President for Instruction: http://www.uga.edu/honesty/.

All FYC students should become very familiar with this site!

Plagiarism

A particular form of academic dishonesty that First-year Composition students need to understand and guard against is plagiarism. *Plagiarism* is the use of another's words or interpretations without giving credit. Plagiarism occurs when writers fail to use quotation marks to indicate exact words from a source, when they fail to paraphrase a passage completely, or when they fail to cite the source of any quotation or paraphrase.

In recent years, cutting and pasting information from the World Wide Web can lead students to commit plagiarism, particularly when they forget where the information was copied from or lose the ability to tell the difference between their own words and those copied from an electronic source. Students should also take particular care to ensure that the Wild Card exhibit for the final electronic portfolio is their own work and identifies correctly any work by other authors included in that piece.

To avoid plagiarism, writers should always:

1. Put quotation marks around any words from sources. When writers use an open book for writing a paper or in taking notes, or when writers take notes by cutting and pasting from an online source or website, they must be careful not to plagiarize unintentionally.

2. Paraphrase material completely; changing or rearranging a few words or the tense of a verb is not paraphrasing. Writers should read the passage to be used, close the source book or minimize the web browser, and then write in their own words what they have read. They should then compare the paraphrase to the source; if by chance key words from the original are included, these should be changed or enclosed in quotation marks.
3. Give accurate and complete citations for all material. *Writer's Help* gives extensive information about MLA documentation style. Writers should refer to this source when creating compositions or should consult with their instructor as to what form is required in a particular course.
4. Avoid borrowing entire arguments or approaches to a subject from another writer. In general, college papers should argue an original idea and should not be paraphrases of another writer's work. All papers that students submit must be their original work. The advantages to writers of a well-documented paper are obvious: documentation shows that writers know their subjects, and the citations give their ideas validity.

Workshop
How Not to Plagiarize

The Provost of the University of Georgia has asked FYC to conduct a program-wide workshop on plagiarism in every ENGL 1101, 1102, and 1103 class in order to support the University of Georgia's efforts to educate students on this subject. The Workshop seeks to inform students about the nature of plagiarism and about ways to avoid plagiarism in their writing. It is designed in two parts, to be completed over two to three class periods, but instructors may wish to complete the entire workshop within one class period. Your teacher will give you specific instructions.

Part 1: Recognizing Plagiarism

1. Read this handout, "**How Not to Plagiarize**," for the Plagiarism Workshop.
2. Review the discussion of "**Academic Honesty and Plagiarism"** in the *First-year Composition Guide, University of Georgia* (Fountainhead Press).
3. On the Web, follow the link to the University of Georgia site on Academic Honesty that is referenced in this section of *First-year Composition Guide*. Review carefully the policies and procedures outlined there.
4. On the Web, go to **The St. Martin's Tutorial on Avoiding Plagiarism.** (See the URL for the website in Works Cited, below). When you log on as a student for the first time, you will be asked for certain information, including the email

address of your instructor so that she or he can receive email reports of your quiz and exercise results. If your instructor wishes for you to provide his or her email and receive your results, she or he will tell you at this time.

5. In *The St. Martin's Tutorial on Avoiding Plagiarism,* read through "**Introduction**" and "**Managing a Project**." Read "**Taking Notes**," but do not complete the accompanying exercises (on summarizing, paraphrasing, and integrating quotations) at this time.
6. In *The St. Martin's Tutorial on Avoiding Plagiarism*, read with special care the section on "**Knowing Which Sources to Acknowledge**." At home/before class, complete the exercise "**Acknowledging Sources**." Be prepared to discuss the results of this exercise and the differences between "common knowledge" and sources that must be acknowledged at your next class meeting.
7. In-class: Discuss Homework results.

Part 2: Acknowledging Sources

1. Review carefully the section on "**Taking Notes**" and read "**Avoiding Plagiarism**" in *The St. Martin's Tutorial on Avoiding Plagiarism*.
2. Complete and submit these exercises: "**Recognizing Summaries**," "**Recognizing Paraphrases,**" "**Avoiding Plagiarism,**" and "**Recognizing Integrated Quotations.**" In your next class meeting, be prepared to discuss the results and implications of these exercises. Be prepared to ask whatever questions you may have about how to avoid plagiarism in summaries and paraphrases and about integrating quotations.

The goals of this Workshop are to support the UGA Academic Honesty Pledge—"I will be academically honest in all of my academic work and will not tolerate academic dishonesty of others"—and to help students use sources wisely in all of their written work.

Resources

Academic Honesty (A Culture of Honesty). Office of the Vice President for Instruction. http://www.uga.edu/honesty/.

First-year Composition at UGA Website. http://english.uga.edu/fyc/pages/1

Price, Margaret. "The St. Martin's Tutorial on Avoiding Plagiarism." Available at http://bcs.bedfordstmartins.com/plagiarismtutorial/.

"*MLA Handbook* Bibliographic Format for References." Research Central. http://www.libs.uga.edu/ref/mlastyle.html.

Resources

8

Students who are new to the University of Georgia are often unsure about what services are available to them and where to go for help of various kinds. This section offers you places to go for help with writing, research, and personal issues.

Tutoring and Help with Writing

The university offers writers in First-year Composition a wide range of services at different locations across campus.

The UGA Writing Center

The Department of English operates the UGA Writing Center in Park Hall 66 as a third-party resource for students looking for help with writing in a 100% confidential space. Undergraduate students, whether in an FYC course or not, are welcome to use its services anytime during their careers at the University of Georgia for up to thirty minutes per week. Serving students and majors across the campus, the Writing Center welcomes all types of writing including but not limited to essays, lab reports, application statements, and CVs/resumes. Common reasons for utilizing the Writing Center include help with content development, overall organization and flow, thesis creation, research, and citations. The Writing Center operates at four additional locations: a satellite center in the Science Library Room 201 (South Campus Writing Center; students with writing for science classes often seek assistance at this location from a Writing Intensive Program consultant with a background in science writing), a location in the Miller Learning Center for after-hours help, a location in the Emma lab in Park Hall 117 (FYC students are encouraged to seek assistance at this location for help with assignments or questions related to Emma and FYC portfolios), and an online consultation service. For hours, policies, and scheduling for all five locations, see the Writing Center's scheduling website at: https://uga.mywconline.com. For general information, see the Center's website: http://writingcenter.english.uga.edu/.

Schedules for the Writing Center are posted by the start of the second week of each academic semester. The Writing Center accepts drop-in clients if no students are scheduled for the desired walk-in time, but scheduling an appointment is the most reliable way to meet with a Writing Center consultant. If you require assistance during the first week of classes, drop-in consultations can occur if there happens to be a consultant available.

Milledge Hall Academic Resource Center

Located in Milledge Hall, the Division of Academic Enhancement provides appointment-based, drop-in, and online tutoring for undergraduate and graduate students across campus and disciplines. Experienced English as a Second Language specialists are available to work in person with multi-lingual students. In addition to Milledge Hall, Academic Enhancement tutoring services are available in the Miller Learning Center and in the South Campus Writing Center, located in the Science Library. For more information, go to the Academic Resource Center: http://tutor.uga.edu/arc/.

Research

One of the biggest changes that students notice in the transition between high school and university is the fact that here they are expected to do research on their own and that they are expected to know how to do quality research in a range of academic disciplines. These are big expectations, but, fortunately, the UGA Libraries can help.

The UGA Libraries

Homepage: http://www.libs.uga.edu

UGA has the largest library in the state with 4.6 million books, thousands of periodical subscriptions, hundreds of online databases, and many librarians to help you navigate through it all. Libraries on campus include:

- Main Library on North Campus: humanities, social sciences, and business;
- Science Library on South Campus: science, technology, and agriculture;
- Miller Learning Center: electronic library resources;
- Special Collections Library: rare books, manuscripts, media archives, and many fascinating exhibits.

For college-level research projects and papers, your instructors will expect you to use *published scholarly* resources and *critically evaluate* any sources you take from the web. Fear not: in addition to its large book collection, the Libraries subscribe to many online databases that include articles and books suitable for college research. Starting at the Libraries' homepage, follow the *Books & More* tab to GIL-Find, the online catalog of books in the UGA Libraries' collections. To find articles from magazines, scholarly journals, and newspapers, start with the default *Multi-Search* tab. Multi-Search lets you limit your results to only full-text articles, only scholarly articles, only newspapers, only ebooks, and other options.

More resources are under the *Articles & Databases* tab:

- *For English 1101*, use ***Academic Search Complete*** for magazine and scholarly journal articles, ***LexisNexis Academic*** for newspaper articles and TV/radio transcripts, and ***CQ Researcher Plus*** for analyses of current issues.

- *For English 1102/1103*, use ***JSTOR*** or the ***MLA International Bibliography*** for literary criticism published in scholarly journals, and ***Literature Resource Center*** for biographies of authors.

Ask a librarian for help choosing keywords, creating a search strategy, and for suggestions for additional discipline-specific databases and resources for your projects.

If you are searching from on campus (including the dorms), you won't need a password to use any of these online resources. To search from off campus, get the password under *GALILEO Password* on the Libraries' homepage.

Need help? Use our "Ask a Librarian" chat box on the library homepage or ask at the reference desk in any of the library buildings. The research support desk at the Main and Science libraries is located on the entry floors; the research support desk at the Miller Learning Center is located at the top of the stairs on the third floor. One-on-one research conferences with librarians are also available; sign up at http://www.libs.uga.edu/ref/instruction/conform.html.

CAPS (Counseling and Psychological Services)

Everyone can use help and support at some time during his or her academic career: "Counseling and Psychiatric Services (CAPS) is dedicated to providing the best available counseling, psychiatric and psychological testing services. CAPS provides short-term individual and couples counseling, group counseling, crisis intervention, medication evaluation and monitoring, psychological testing, and makes referrals to resources on and off-campus when appropriate" (http://www.uhs.uga.edu/caps/). For more information, call 706-542-2273 or see the website from which this text was taken: http://www.uhs.uga.edu/caps/.

Whatever assistance you need, you can find it at the University of Georgia. If you are having problems—whether personal or academic—you can also ask your teacher for a referral to the proper resource.

What Comes Next?

9

Research into the writing process shows that the use of writing as a part of the learning process and frequency of writing are both crucial to improving and maintaining the writing skills and critical thinking processes that students acquire in their First-year Composition classes. What is more, employers consistently report on the importance of basic communication skills, especially in writing, for the workplace. Research has also suggested a close connection between reading and writing proficiency, and UGA students have shown that they enjoy reading and discussing books outside their formal classes. For all of these reasons, the University of Georgia encourages you to seek out other opportunities for practice in reading and writing. We would like to conclude by telling you about future opportunities to practice your literacy skills and to use writing as a powerful learning tool.

Writing Certificate Program

The University of Georgia offers an interdisciplinary certificate program in writing. The purpose of the Writing Certificate Program is to give undergraduate students from all colleges and majors at the University of Georgia an opportunity to develop and document their writing skills as they move from First-year Composition through the core curriculum and their academic majors en route to further education, professional training, or the workplace. Their writing skills will be developed in the context of their particular academic studies and interests and will be documented in a capstone electronic portfolio that presents and reflects on the students' writing projects and experiences throughout their undergraduate career. The writing done for the program will enhance students' understanding in their chosen field of study and will provide evidence to outside evaluators (such as admissions committees or employers) of the students' critical thinking, research, and communication skills, plus their understanding of genres and conventions of writing within their chosen discipline. For more information about the program and its benefits, visit: http://ctl.uga.edu/teaching-resources/writing_certificate.

Writing Intensive Program (WIP)

The Writing Intensive Program at the University of Georgia offers students multiple opportunities to strengthen their writing throughout their undergraduate experience by offering writing-intensive courses throughout the university in varying disciplines—from Art History to Biology to Music to Sociology, for example. A key goal of the program is to foster student writing *in the disciplines*, by helping students understand the conventions—or "ways of knowing"—of a particular discipline: how knowledge is constructed and communicated, and what rules of evidence and argumentation are practiced. To accomplish the goals of the program, each Writing Intensive Program (WIP) course is supported by a specially trained "writing coach," who works with students to improve their writing and performance in the course by providing constructive and personal feedback. The advantages of this coaching—and WIP courses, in general—are many. A compelling majority of students enrolled in these courses consistently report that their experience with the Writing Intensive Program strengthened their writing skills; built their confidence in the writing process; encouraged a deeper engagement in course reading, discussions, and assignments; taught them the writing conventions of their discipline; heightened their critical thinking skills; and prepared them for writing in other courses and future goals, such as graduate school or career-related work. **All WIP courses count toward requirements for the Writing Certificate Program**.

For more information about the program and its benefits, as well as for a list of current WIP courses, visit: http://**www.wip.uga.edu.**

The Major and Minor in English

The skills in writing and critical thinking that you have learned in First-year Composition will serve you well if you decide to major or minor in English. English majors learn to read, interpret, and analyze texts (novels, stories, plays, films, poems, essays, images, and other forms of cultural production) and to write with poise, brevity, and elegance. Majors can choose Areas of Emphasis for their Program of Study; Areas of Emphasis include Creative Writing, American Literature, Multicultural American Literature, Rhetoric and Composition, Humanities Computing, Medieval Literature, Studies in the Novel, Poetics, Advanced Studies in English, Interdisciplinary Renaissance Studies, and English Language Studies. Majors and minors can go on to careers in almost anything: teaching, publishing, law, journalism, management, human resources, business communication, medicine, grant-writing, screen-writing, technical writing, and so on. Employers take an English major or minor as evidence of strong skills in writing, creativity, and critical thinking. You can find more information about the English major and minor at the program website: http://www.english.uga.edu/newsite/undergrad/home.html.

Declared English majors may join the Student Advisory Council, "SAC," and help plan events such as graduation and our new undergraduate speaker series, "Life after Park Hall." Contact the Undergraduate English Office in Park 111 for more information.

Advanced Courses in Writing

The English Department offers several upper-division courses in writing that are open to students in other majors. The Academic Enhancement Program, housed in Milledge Hall, also offers an array of writing classes for native and non-native speakers.

UNIV 1105. Improving Grammar, Usage, and Style.
3 hours.

This course teaches students to master formal grammar rules and terminology, to achieve a clear, fluent writing style, and to recognize common problems of usage so that they can effectively write and edit papers for academic and professional audiences.

Note: Students may enroll in this course simultaneously with ENGL 1101.

UNIV 1115. Introduction to Academic Writing.
3 hours (institutional credit).

The objective of the course is to prepare students for the kinds of writing required in English 1101 and other University courses. To meet that objective, UNIV 1115 stresses strategies for generating ideas and improving writing fluency, conventions of academic usage and style, patterns for organizing thought and arranging written material, and critical thinking and analysis. In the classroom and in individualized instruction, students receive extensive practice drafting, editing, and revising expository and persuasive essays.

Note: This course carries institutional credit and will not count toward graduation.

UNIV 1117. Basic Composition for Multilingual Writers.
3 hours (institutional credit).

This course is designed for both undergraduate and graduate students whose first language is not English. Its objectives include mastering English grammar, idioms, and sentence structure; building an academic vocabulary; and composing short academic papers. The course emphasizes problems that non-native speakers typically experience with proofreading, revision, and writing for an American audience. Assignments may be tailored to students' majors.

Note: This course carries institutional credit and will not count toward graduation.

ENGL 3590. Technical Communication.
3 hours.

This course deals with writing in the professional domains, with an emphasis on research methods, clear and accurate presentation of ideas and data, and computer-mediated communication. If you want an introduction to the role of writing in the workplace, this course would be for you.

ENGL 3600. Advanced Composition.
3 hours.

Advanced Composition focuses less on professional contexts than on writing as a process, with an emphasis on the conventions of discourse situations, invention, revision, editorial skills, and document design. This course is particularly useful for students who want to practice and improve their academic writing.

ENGL 4832. Writing for the World Wide Web.
3 hours.

This class deals with both the theory and practice of writing for the World Wide Web. Here you will learn to use the basic tools to construct web sites and be introduced to other advanced technologies useful for academic and professional writers.

ENGL 4833. Composition Theory and Pedagogy.
3 hours.

This course introduces you to the history and theories of college composition teaching. With a strong practical emphasis, ENGL 4833 prepares students to work as college writing tutors or as classroom writing assistants.

Donald E. Barnett Awards for 2014-2015

10

Donald E. Barnett Awards for 2014-2015

Each year, the First-year Composition Program recognizes excellent writing in English 1101, 1102, and 1103 by presenting three Barnett Awards. Named in honor of Donald E. Barnett, who directed the Freshman English Program for many years, the awards consist of cash prizes and publication of the winning compositions in the *First-year Composition Guide* required of all students registered in our courses and on the FYC site at: http://www.english.uga.edu/newsite/fyc/barnett.html.

Scott Davis

Albert Dixon

English 1101

19 September 2014

Fine, whatever....

In the digital age, expressing your emotion can be as easy as typing one or two punctuation characters, such as a colon and parentheses to make a smiley face :). You have probably seen this string of characters or other ones like it various times throughout texting, email, IM messaging, or other examples of CMC (computer-mediated communication), but where did it all come from? CMC is essentially any human communication that occurs by two or more electronic devices ("Computer-mediated communication"), which would inherently include texting. The character shown above, as well as :(:-) :-(:P :/ and many others, is an example of "letters" or "configurations" in the alphabet of emoticons. However, perhaps the "emoji," easily considered emoticon 2.0, is of more importance and weight in today's communications, as it is more modern: ☺ ☹. Although you, the reader, may not be *as* familiar with these as you are with emoticons, you have still

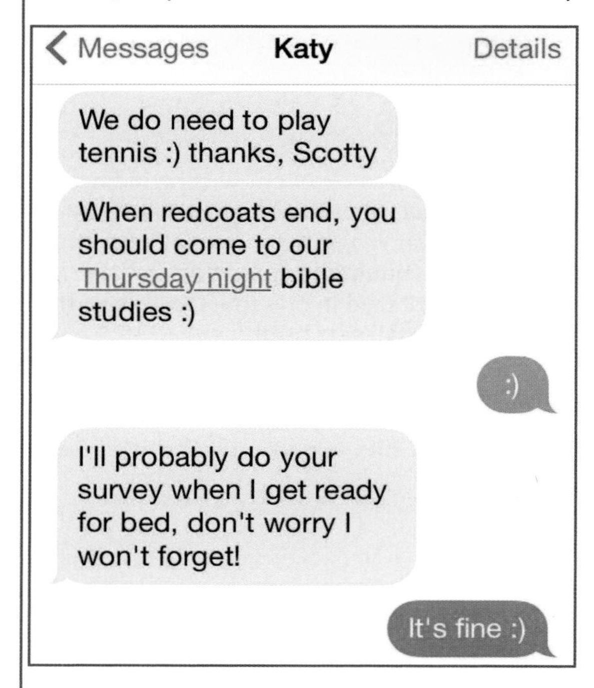

likely seen them by some form of CMC. While most people over the age of 25 likely think of emoticons and emojis as pointless and as adding little meaning to writing (Marsden 2), these characters have a big effect on today's CMC, especially emotionally. In fact, they were made explicitly for emotional expression, created to fill the emotional, tonal, and modal hole that had been created naturally in CMC. Additionally, long before the emoticon, ever since writing was established, we have had punctuation as a writing tool to help establish tone and emotion. In a world of short and brief text messages, punctuation and emojis/emoticons determine the tone of the text message more than the actual words do. This makes the textual interaction more human and allows us to communicate more naturally as well as personally by allowing us to add visual components of communication that were originally lost.

With the kind of language we use in texting, the words themselves alone lack effective tone. Critics of the emoticon and emoji claim that they reduce writing and emotional intelligence, but this is a biased and superficial criticism that often seeks to compare CMC with formal writing. Alice Robb, one such critic, states that "the ability to convey tone and emotion through text, without resorting to illustration, is one of the key challenges of writing. It's what makes someone a good writer rather than an effective artist or illustrator" (4). The problem with this reasoning is that formal writing is a very different type of communication and text than computer-mediated communication. Formal writing is generally longer and the writing itself is much further planned out than that of CMC. Formal writing attempts to make fantastic literature through thought-out, revised, and doubly revised word content, while CMC's purpose is to represent common, everyday conversation within the digital world of text. Most people do not just walk around reciting poetry as means of conversation, and in the same way, CMC exists to represent not literature, but conversation.

People soon discovered a problem with the invention of CMC, however. This problem was that while the text of CMC could accurately represent the words of conversation, certain characteristics of normal human conversation, such as audio tone and visual cues, had been lost (Sherwood 1). In fact, statistically, 93% of human communication occurs visually through body language and through tone of voice (Harmon 70). This is where the emoticon comes in. Judith

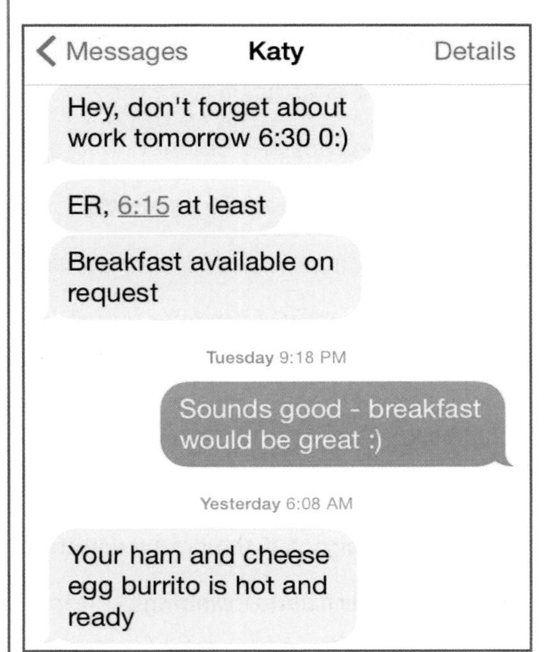

Meyer says, “Nowadays, we often use writing as a form of quick communication in text messages and chats. These don’t leave the time to carefully consider how we can avoid misunderstandings of our tone, so emoticons are a very useful tool.” With the help of the emoticon, we are able to clarify emotional context with what would have been otherwise

ambiguous emotional standing within a message, as well as make text messaging more human. Take, for example, the text message displayed on the previous page, from a friend of mine to me. She started the conversation with, “Hey, don’t forget about work tomorrow 6:30 0:)”, reminding me to give her a ride to work. However, if she had said the same phrase without the smiley face featuring a halo, the message could have come across as selfish, nagging, and possibly even condescending. With the addition of a simple smiley face, especially an angelic reference of innocence, I know that she is kindly reminding me and is thankful for my giving her a ride. Clarifying emotional context is important, both in personal communications as well as business communications, not only to further express what is meant, but even more importantly to make sure that the message is not misinterpreted tonally (Sherwood 1, 7). Judith Meyer says that “[t]he faster the communication, the more acceptable is the use of emoticons. In chats and SMS they are very acceptable and have prevented some big misunderstandings.”

Punctuation also helps clarify tone and emotional ground in text messaging, but some of the punctuation marks are beginning to take on new meanings with new tone and significance.

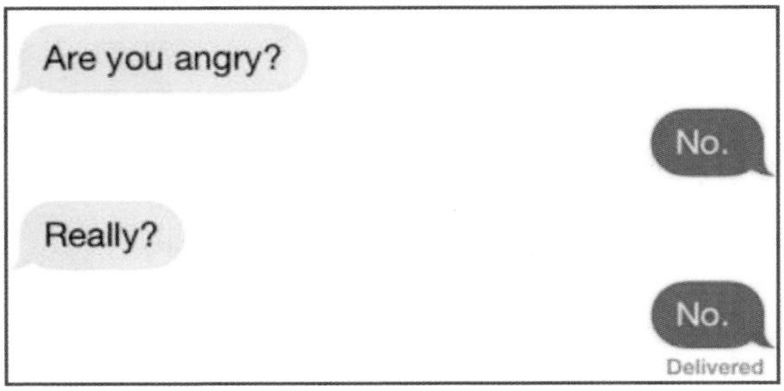

In text messaging the characteristics of brevity, speed, and simplicity are the name of the game, and with this purpose much punctuation is often dropped, leading to many punctuation marks acquiring new meanings. The primary and most important example is the period. The line break has replaced the period as a separator of speech, and the period has slowly shifted to accept a new meaning (Crair 2). Additionally, "The unpunctuated, un-ended sentence is incredibly addicting," says Choire Sicha, editor of the *Awl*. "I feel liberated to make statements without that emphasis, and like I'm continuing the conversation, even when I'm definitely not" (qtd. in Crair 2). In text messaging and even in IM messages, the default way to end your phrase is to just end it, no period involved. I mean, why would we use a period when everything we are typing is usually one sentence and is just meant to represent conversation? Thus, since the appearance of a period is rare in the texting world, it adds new meaning when it is used because the reader tries to figure out why it was used. The period is not used as a punctuation mark anymore but rather as a tone differential, subliminal message, or indication of the end of the conversation (not just the sentence) (Crair 3). That tone differential has come to have a negative connotation, usually either to indicate that the writer is upset, angry, or another similar emotion. Ben Crair explains that "people use the period not simply to conclude a sentence, but to announce 'I am not happy about the sentence I just concluded'"(1). It is truly an amazing innovation, in that a punctuation mark that was used to express separation and pause in speaking and literature has now adapted to indicate tone (Crair 3).

What this all means is that people have over time developed a completely different language than that of standard conversation to be used in CMC, specifically in text messaging. The visual letters of the alphabet are emoticons and emojis, the words of the alphabet are standard English words (although many have been abbreviated or made acronymic), and the audio letters of the alphabet are punctuation marks that have taken on a new meaning in the world of CMC. Tom Fanelli refers to this adaptation as "a new set of communicative dimensions that haven't [sic] existed in the past. This kind of light-speed evolution of our language will only accelerate as technology advances and becomes further integrated into our way of life" (2). It is not just the period, either. As far as punctuation goes, another example is the exclamation point, which has turned into a sincerity marker: "I really mean what I am saying!" This change in meaning for the

exclamation marker is also due to tonal ambiguity, specifically whether a message is relayed as sarcastic or not. The new role for the exclamation mark was created to leave no room for sarcastic ambiguity (Crair 4). Ben Crair states that "as problems of tone kept arising on text and instant message, people turned to other punctuation marks on their keyboards rather than inventing new ones" (4), which is what led to punctuation acquiring new meanings in computer-mediated communication. One final example on the punctuation side is the ellipsis mark. In traditional writing, an ellipsis is used to indicate trailing away, uncertainty, etc. In the CMC world, however, the ellipsis mark has come to mean a secret message. That secret message could be in the form of reading between the lines to figure out something the texter was trying to say without actually saying it (Greenspan 12), or it could be in the form of a more quiet and open-ended negativity similar to the period (Crair 4).

The unique CMC language does not stop with punctuation in what it has altered either. Two popular examples of this include "K" and "fine." Of course, if the newly declared sincerity marker is used after these expressions, then the meaning is parallel with that of standard English. When it is not is when the two

expressions can mean something entirely different, especially with the addition of the period. "K" is one simple letter and was created as a simple shorter version of "ok," but in the world of text messaging, it can be loaded with lots of different meanings. The general sense of meaning, however, is that of detachment. "K," when used in the evolving new CMC definition of the phrase, is almost always not positive (and usually negative), and the possible modes of detachment could include disinterest, depression, annoyance, anger, frustration, or one of many other emotions. The latter of the two expressions, "fine," is very similar, although it is usually used in the depression realm to actually talk about not being fine. However, "fine" has almost been evolving both in spoken conversation as well as typed conversation at the same time since its origin, so this is not a language change unique to CMC.

Even more interesting than the ways that the emoticon and emoji enhance texting and tone is how it does so. It enhances and supplements tone through a simulated visual representation of ourselves. Words are words, punctuation functions as audio tone, and then emoticons and emojis work to bring about the visual aspect of the conversation. Chad Tossell states that emoticons are "[s]imilar to facial expressions and other non-verbal communications" (et al. 660), and I would venture to say that the link between the two is closer than we think. As we type out a text message, our facial expression is expressed through a facial icon on our correspondent's screen, showing that person what we looked like visually as we read and replied to (or simply sent) the message. Take, for example, the difference in use between men and women. The common consensus across most women and men is that women are normally more emotional and expressive than men. In text messaging, we see the exact same thing as we study amounts of emoticons and emojis sent by females as compared to males (Tossell et al. 659, 662). This in turn shows that emoticons and emojis are a natural representation of ourselves, work effectively, and make text messaging a more human and interactive experience. But, do emoticons, emojis, and punctuation really work as well as we want them to?

The simple and short answer is yes. The emoticon, emoji, and use of punctuation all have great effect emotionally and tonally on text messaging. However,

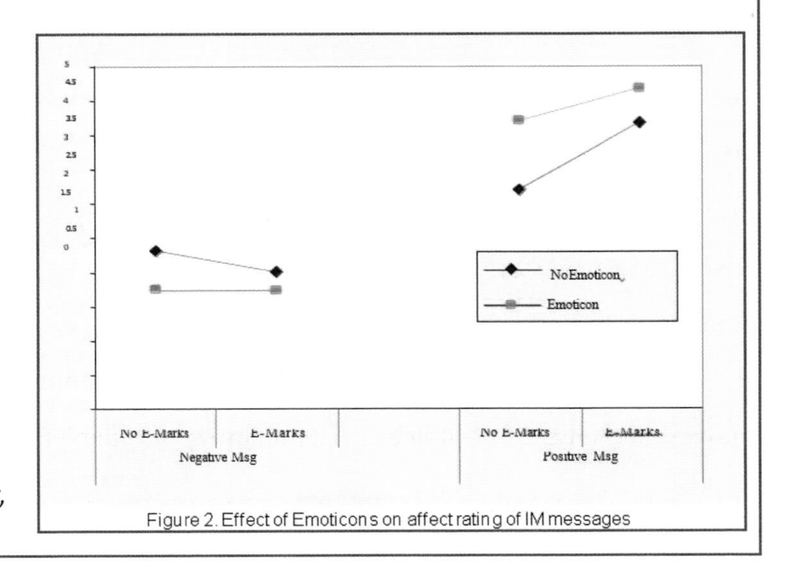

Figure 2. Effect of Emoticons on affect rating of IM messages

when emoticons/emojis and punctuation are used together as opposed to when they are not makes for a very interesting relationship. Take, for example, the graph above, which plots the emotional and tonal effect of emoticons and exclamation marks. Interestingly enough, if you are trying to portray a negative message, your best bet is to use an emoticon. However, if you use an exclamation mark without an emoticon, your negative effect will go up, and if you use an emoticon to start with, you will have an already more negative effect, but it will not change if you add any exclamation marks. On the other hand, if you are trying to portray a positive message, your best bet is to use both an emoticon and exclamation mark. Without the emoticon, the addition of the exclamation point makes a huge jump in effect, and with the emoticon, the effect already starts quite high and then rises more from there (Ip 2). Amy Ip additionally says, "The results of this study show that, despite the simplicity and brevity of IM messages, emoticons and punctuation marks can make a significant difference in how people interpret the message" (2).

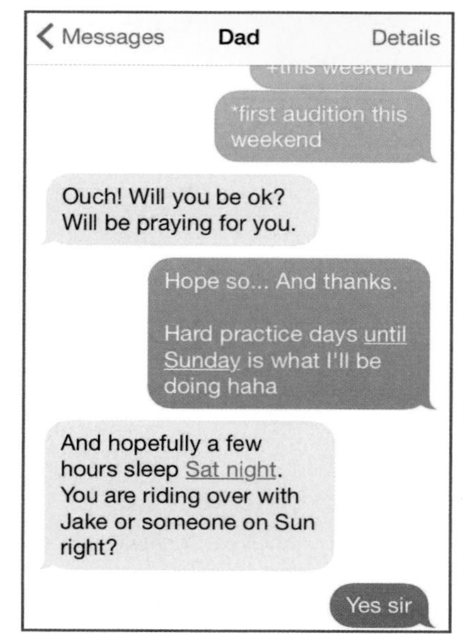

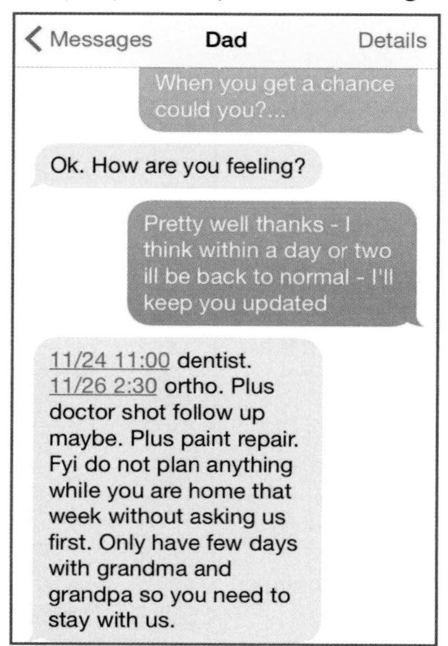

However, effect is a very general term, and it applies to different people in different ways. In relation to emoticons and emojis, different emoticons and especially emojis can have different effects based on with whom they are used. Alice Rob explains, “Friend groups fall into the habit of using certain emoticons, just as they develop their own slang” (2). A particular group of friends may stumble

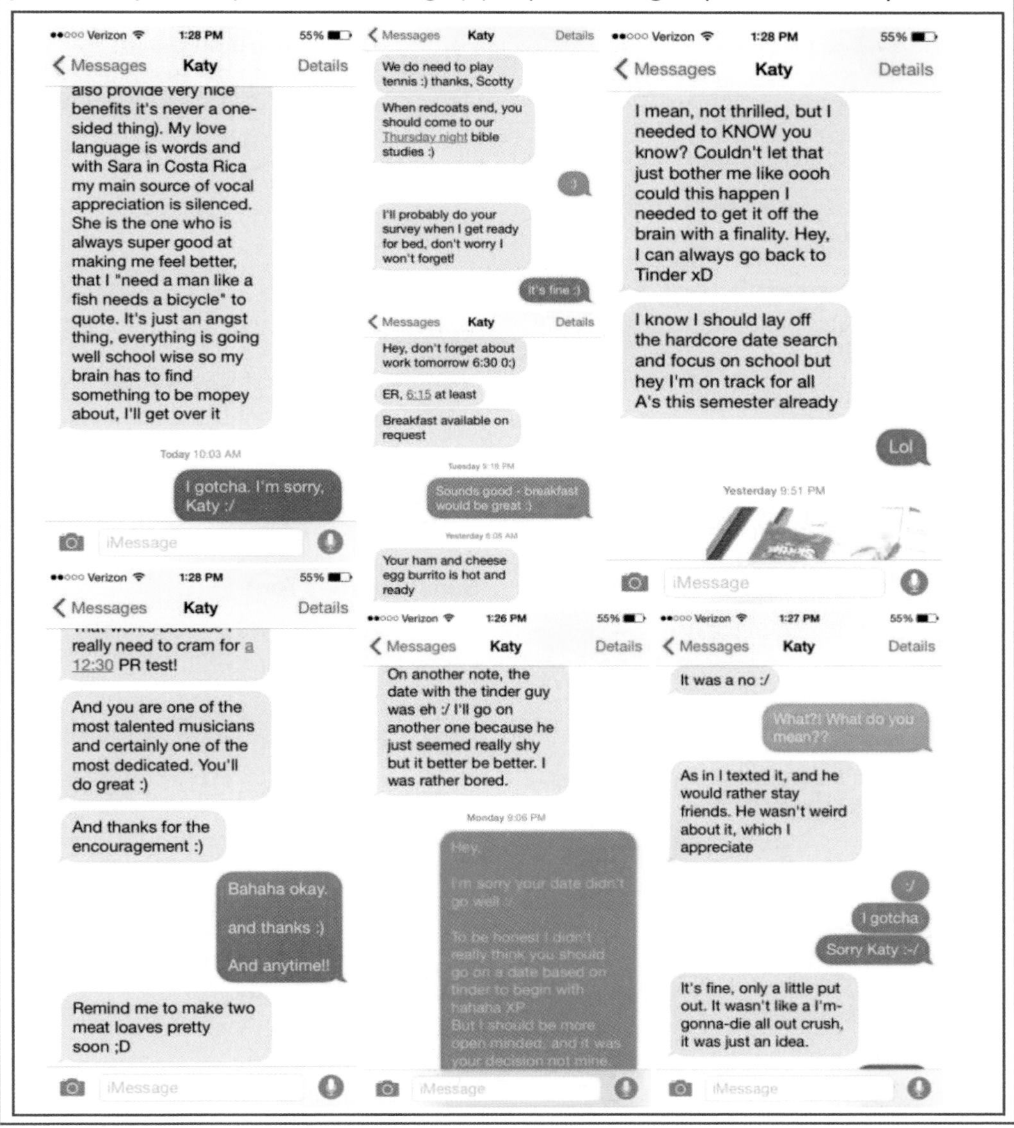

upon an emoji that means nothing to them literally but becomes almost like an inside joke, and therefore sticks. So while the CMC language is changing as a whole, that change is different based on the groups involved. For example, when I text my dad, he texts as though it were normal writing: punctuation used for original purposes, usually not many emoticons, and just typing things out (and not trying to

sound sarcastic or disconnected or anything negative in the process). When I text my friend Katy, there is a certain set of emoticons that we normally use with just each other because they describe our conversation and friendship best. Finally, when I text my girlfriend, there is also a certain set of emojis that we use between us way more than the others, because over time we have developed our own CMC dialect, just like every group has done over time.

All in all, computer-mediated communication requires something additional as it represents everyday conversation in short bursts of text. CMC lacks the visual and audio components of conversation that we have face-to-face, and therefore it is hard to express these parts of conversation that directly lead to overall tone. Because of this difference, the emoticon and emoji were invented and have served well to enhance tone in texting by representing people visually. This usage has led to text messaging becoming more human and becoming a more natural extension of our everyday conversation. For the audio components of everyday speech, we use punctuation, some of which we use with new definitions exclusively for CMC, such as the period and ellipsis mark. These techniques have been effective, and they work because they parallel our actual understanding of conversation and provide a good substitution for such elements in the text world. Additionally, the changing language of CMC, which has evolved to adapt visual and audio "letters," has been further extended into innumerable dialects created by the fact that there are many different groups of people, all different in connections among one another. It seems that we as a people are beginning to speak a foreign language without even realizing it.

Works Cited

"Computer-mediated Communication." *Wikipedia*. Wikimedia Foundation, 17 Nov. 2014. Web. 19 Nov. 2014.

Crair, Ben. "The Period Is Pissed: When did our plainest punctuation mark become so aggressive?" *Newrepublic.com*. The New Republic, 25 Nov. 2013. Web. 19 Nov. 2014.

Fanelli, Tom. "The Evolution of Human Communication: Emoticons, Internet Slang, and Texting." *Tom Fanelli*. N.p., 10 Feb. 2013. Web. 19 Nov. 2014.

Finn, T. Andrew. *Emoticons*. University Web Space. George Mason University, n.d. Web. 19 Nov. 2014.

Gacey, Hannah, Lisa Moore, and Jim Gallo. "Some SCIENCE Behind the Smiley... Emoticons and Their Possible Impact on the Workplace." *HR Florida Review*. HR Florida State Council, 23 Oct. 2013. Web. 19 Nov. 2014.

Greenspan, Sam. "11 Secret Meanings Behind Punctuation in Text Messages." *Wired.com*. Conde Nast Digital, 7 June 2011. Web. 19 Nov. 2014.

Harmon, Patricia. "Does Texting Affect Emotional Intelligence?" *T+D* 67.7 (2013): 70-71. *Academic Search Complete*. Web. 19 Nov. 2014.

Ip, Amy. "The Impact of Emoticons on Affect Interpretation in Instant Messaging." *AmySmile*. N.p., n.d. Web. 19 Nov. 2014.

Marsden, Rhodri. "More than Words: Are 'emoji' Dumbing Us down or Enriching Our Communications?" *TheIndependent*.com. Independent Digital News and Media, 13 May 2013. Web. 19 Nov. 2014.

Meyer, Judith. "Is the Use of Emojis and Emoticons a More Effective Way to Communicate Tone than Text Alone, or Is Their Use a Sign of Inadequate Writing Skill?" *Quora.com.* N.p. 16 Feb. 2014. Web. 19 Nov. 2014.

Robb, Alice. "How Using Emoji Makes Us Less Emotional." *Newrepublic.com*. The New Republic, Web. 19 Nov. 2014.

Sherwood, Kaitlin. "Chapter 8 - Convey Emotional Tone." *Overcome Email Overload with Eudora 5*. N.p., 2001. Web. 19 Nov. 2014.

Steinmetz, Katy. "Not Just A Smiley Face." *Time* 184.4 (2014): 52-53. *Academic Search Complete*. Web. 19 Nov. 2014.

Tossell, Chad C., et al. "A Longitudinal Study Of Emoticon Use In Text Messaging From Smartphones." *Computers In Human Behavior* 28.2 (2012): 659-663. *Academic Search Complete*. Web. 19 Nov. 2014.

Wortham, Jenna. "Online Emotions, in Hundreds of New Flavors." *New York Times* 10 Mar. 2013: 3. *Academic Search Complete*. Web. 19 Nov. 2014.

Brian West

Raffaela Wilson

ENGL 1102

18 November 2014

Dealing with Damaged Relationships

Damaged relationships, especially those between close family members, are often never repaired. Unfortunately, this damage commonly leads to a situation in which one is left alone to reconcile after the other has passed. Those who have experienced this situation know the difficulty of accepting and forgiving. Lucille Clifton, in her poem "forgiving my father," and Theodore Roethke, in his poem "My Papa's Waltz," explore their own turbulent relationships with their fathers. Both poets comment on the painful nature of these relationships and use writing as a means of reconciliation. The two styles, which include a resentful confrontation and an ambiguous narrative, show the versatility of this process.

The diction Clifton uses demands a response; she shows clearly the pain her father caused her. She uses the metaphor of financial debt to reveal her feelings of being owed, calling on her father to make a payment that is overdue. She calls to her father to reconcile: "today is payday, payday old man" (line 5). She yearns to collect the repayment of the emotional deficit with which she was left. She also uses this metaphor to show how she eventually concedes to her father's passing. She uses an eerie metaphor for her father's coffin, commenting on "debtor's boxes," for which "no accounting will open them up" (22-23). With this metaphor, Clifton reveals that she accepts that her father has moved on, even if the debt has not been collected. Though she is left to endure the anguish left by her father, lamenting over his passing only causes more agony.

Unlike Clifton's address to her father, "My Papa's Waltz" narrates a memory of Roethke's childhood, and he does not directly address his father. The ambiguity of the poem's plot leaves the reader to deduce its meaning. However, one aspect is clear; Roethke wants to reveal something about his relationship with his father. In order to determine exactly what his meaning is, one must consider the writer's intention. If Roethke intended on simply commenting on the abuse, which could be physical or emotional, he would have no reason to hide his feelings. Because of this more complicated notion of addressing the issue so that he can reconcile, he uses phrases which could be argued as specific instances of abuse or written off as part of a playful game: "We romped until the pans / Slid from the kitchen shelf" and "You beat time on my head / With a palm caked by dirt" (5-6, 13-14). His ambiguity attempts to explain the complex division of emotions that he feels for his father. Clearly, his father's actions have caused discontent for Roethke, but the indirect style in which he reveals this suggests that he wishes to protect the memory of his father. Though it is not actively expressed in the text, Roethke begins a notion of approval of his father with this nod toward protecting his memory. In this manner, Roethke shows a method of reconciliation which contrasts with Clifton's direct style.

Both poets offer a commentary on their emotions using tone and syntax. "forgiving my father" is a carefully constructed and meticulous response to complex emotion. The text is aggressively directed; Clifton speaks personally to her father, calling him "old man" and "old pauper old prisoner, old dead man" (5,

20). The overarching tone of the piece is, at first, pained and unforgiving. However, it should be noted that this is not the only voice that Clifton uses. The poem, and even the title, are notably written in lower case, which gives the author's voice a soft spoken, almost apologetic tone. "My Papa's Waltz" employs a much different approach. In his poem, Roethke presents a narrative that is purposefully ambiguous. He does not make clear whether the plot actually alludes to a dance that he and his father once shared or an instance of abuse. A case could certainly be made for either side. He begins with "The whiskey on your breath / Could make a small boy dizzy," which sets a dark and strident initial tone (1-2). The tone subtly shifts throughout the work to one that is more affectionate and pure. Toward the end, he remarks that after the events of the night, the father "waltzed me off to bed / Still clinging to [his] shirt" (15-16). This change in the author's portrayal of his father indicates that he, like Clifton, has competing emotions of resentment and compassion.

As we read closer, we find that Clifton uses a similar strategy, as she hints at possible conflicted emotion. While her language is harsh and her attitude toward her father is bitter, she hints that this may not be her sole sentiment. Immediately following a comment about her feeling of being owed, she presents a statement which appears to counter her demands of reconciliation. She admits to her father that "you were the son of a needy father, / the father of a needy son" (12-13). She goes on to concede that "you gave her all you had / which was nothing. You have already given her / all you had" (14-16). These words, especially when read aloud in the reserved, anguished tone that the lower case style proposes, plainly reveal Clifton's alternate emotions. Within these lines, she admits to a justification that she may need if she is to truly forgive her father. Similarly, Roethke uses diction to indicate his willingness to accept his father's flaws by identifying positive aspects of their relationship. He does this primarily by alluding to the father's role as a caretaker. He mentions his father's "palm caked hard by dirt" (14). When considering that the father's work entailed tending to a large greenhouse, the reader surmises that this is not a disapproving remark about the father's hygiene, but rather an admiration of his exhausting labor. Through this remark, Roethke, like Clifton, deftly and skillfully presents himself with justification for his father's behavior. Here, the reader begins to see the hints of forgiveness and the implication of reconciliation

In essence, "forgiving my father" is a personal exploration of resentment with undertones of forgiveness and compassion, while "My Papa's Waltz" is an affectionate narrative with conflicted feelings of animosity and regret. Each poem has a unique delivery, but neither appears to be distinctly less effective than the other in its purpose. Both poets eventually reach a resolution that is at least productive, if not satisfying. To these poets, it seems that merely talking about their problems is enough to elicit improvement. The authors prove to the reader that this type of cognitive process is worth the pain that it sometimes entails. Though it is often difficult, relationships can be mended, as Roethke and Clifton demonstrate, if one makes a substantial and impartial attempt at forgiveness.

Works Cited

Clifton, Lucille. "forgiving my father." *Making Literature Matter: An Anthology for Readers and Writers*. Ed. John Schilb and John Clifford. Boston: Bedford/St. Martin's, 2012. 270-71. Print.

Roethke, Theodore. "My Papa's Waltz." *Making Literature Matter: An Anthology for Readers and Writers*. Ed. John Schilb and John Clifford. Boston: Bedford/St. Martin's, 2012. 273. Print.

Michael G. Moran Electronic Portfolio Awards for 2014-2015

Michael G. Moran Awards for 2014-2015

Beginning in 2007, the First-year Composition Program began recognizing the excellent work being done in electronic portfolios for English 1101, 1102, and 1103 by presenting three portfolio awards. Named in honor of Michael G. Moran, a former director of FYC who did much to shape and improve the program, the awards consist of cash prizes and publication in the *First-year Composition Guide* required of all students registered in our courses and on the FYC site at: http://www.english.uga.edu/newsite/fyc/moran.html.

English 1101

Student: Alyssa Shrewsbury

Alyssa Shrewsbury's passion for art permeates her ePortfolio. Conveying an exceptional sense of unity, Alyssa's exhibits not only focus on art as subject matter (as in her essays), but also compare the composing processes of the artist and the writer. Her Revision and Peer Review pieces offer particularly compelling analogies between creating visual art and the experience of process writing in her composition course. Finally, Alyssa's use of images—from famous works of art, galleries around Athens, and her own work—makes for a visually exciting ePortfolio.

Living By a New Title

Art has always been my hobby, but for me, viewing myself as an artist was intimidating and required me to change my perception of who an artist could be. I had it built up in my mind that only one kind of person could be an artist and because I did not fit the stereotypical portrayal of a moody, recluse hipster carrying around a mug of herbal tea at all times, who was I to pretend that I was an artist? This disconnect between who I am and what I do not only restricted my ability to create, but also obscured my perception of who I could be. It was not until two summers ago when I visited the High Museum of Art that I was able to take on the title of an artist.

This is the self portrait of Rembrandt that I saw at the High Museum of Art.

During my visit, the featured artist was Johannes Vermeer. He is best know for the masterpiece *The Girl With the Pearl Earring*. With such a famous and mysterious work on display, I did not expect a quiet self-portrait by Rembrandt to engage and inspire me the most that day. The plaque by Rembrandt's self-portrait described how he was perceived in his day.

Rembrandt was known for being fun and outgoing. He was, simply put, a lover of life. Thinking about the words on the plaque, I realized something that I was never able to admit it to myself before: I felt unworthy to be called an artist.

Rembrandt's portrait helped me to shed my previous interpretation of who an artist could be and gave me the freedom to consider myself as one. On a wider scope, I learned that people should not restrict who they are because of what they do. By now considering myself an artist, I have a genuine creative voice and am an honest risk taker. My work no longer reflects what I think an artist would create. Rather, my personal voice is the only prevailing factor in my art. Rembrandt's strength was his different perspective on life. Art was a way for him to reflect and inspire viewers to live with the same vigor and enthusiasm as he did. In the same way, my positive perspective and ability to feel something without relying on a moody personality only strengthens my creative voice and sets my work apart. My goal is to use personal experiences and my unique perspective to inspire viewers and help them gain insight. By stepping into a new identity for myself, my viewers can consider my work through the honesty it sets forth.

This photo was taken the day I visited the High Museum of Art.

Works Cited

Harmenszoon van Rijn, Rembrandt. *Self-Portrait with Lace Collar*. c. 1629. Web Gallery of Art. *www.wga.hu.* Web. 8 Dec. 2014.

Shrewsbury, Alyssa. *Another Girl With a Pearl Earring*. 2014. Photograph.

Shrewsbury, Alyssa. *Self-Portrait with milkshake*. 2014. Charcoal.

Where Art and Writing Meet: Problem Solving

Whenever I create something, regardless of if I am confident in my ability to be successful or not, there is a sense of urgency that goes through my head. A blank canvas is not always an invitation to free my thoughts and let loose; it is a problem that I must solve. There is a point, however, when I realize that relying on my instincts has paid off and I know that the piece is headed in good direction. When I started English 1101 at the beginning of this semester, I was greatly intimidated as I had never considered myself a writer. If I perceived a blank canvas as a problem, a blank word document felt like an impossible feat to overcome. However, I found that I approach and resolve papers much in the same way that I approach and resolve my art. In order to display how my being an artist resonates with my writing, each of my essay topics and what I learned during the writing process revolve around the idea that creating art is really problem solving.

When writing my first paper, my strength was the motives behind my words. I focused on fashioning out my ideas and felt for the first time my writing could accomplish something. Whereas before I was assigned to write on things that seemed trivial and unimportant, I now felt that someone could read my work and actually gain something from it. That was exciting for me. I remember walking back to my dorm after receiving the prompt for my first paper. My mind was ferociously conjuring up thoughts of all that I wanted to address in this first paper. All of a sudden I wanted to make a statement about who I was, and now I was able to do it.

Writing is a way of defending who I am as a person. In a way, it proves the big, exciting ideas in my mind are in fact my own because I am able to show the intricate trek it took me to make those conclusions. When writing my first paper, I was excited to have a voice and speak up about something that directly related to me. Whereas before I had always used art as a way to express my feelings, writing now gave me a new way to explicitly say how I felt about a topic.

For me, the problem of writing does not reside in the inspiration, but in the execution. I was perplexed as I had so many thoughts but no way of unpacking them in a way that made sense. It felt like I had all the pieces to a puzzle and yet had no idea how to fit them together so that they formed a proper essay. This is often the sense I feel when approaching my canvas. I feel pressured because I am passionate about what I intend to create and want to do it justice. As I had sat unable to write an entire paragraph for too long, I started throwing out single sentences and phrases I knew I wanted to include in some way. It was not too long before I was able to connect my ideas and guide the reader through my thought process. Sure it was messy at first, but that is often the way I approach my writing and my art. It feels less intimidating to set down those dirtier colors and build up the entire painting together. This way I don't get caught up in making the image perfect to begin with and lose sight of my passion for the idea I am conveying through my art. In the same way, when approaching my first paper, I threw out what I had: messy ideas that didn't necessarily relate to one another or make sense. As a writer and an artist, it is my duty to address the problem by creating work that is unified and maintains the passion I had going into the project.

My second paper's strength is that it shows how I can incorporate many sources into a paper that can be still be followed and make sense. The task seemed daunting as I had to include two separate field studies, an interview, and a preface referencing a completely separate work of art into a single paper. I was perplexed about how I could string together so many ideas in a way that fit together to form a proper essay. My writing process was very messy as it required me to constantly move around sections of my paper until I had created an order I was satisfied with. I was dead set on referencing the statue *Aphrodite of Knidos* at the beginning and end of my paper as her story encompasses the importance of art's orientation — the thesis of the paper. Although she added another element to an already broad paper in terms of outside sources, I felt that she strengthened my coherence by framing my ideas as she was referenced from beginning to end. I considered leaving this work of art out of my paper, but in the end, she is a testament to how writing, much like art, has to be worked out. In the end, I was rewarded in seeing how I wascapable of blending many elements into a cohesive final product.

When creating my wildcard, I knew that I wanted to incorporate some of my own art, but more importantly, present it in a new way. By making an artist statement, I was able to inject life and meaning into my work. Whereas before my art had to speak for itself, my voice as an artist was strengthened with the addition of my writing voice. After I had completed the painting and was left to write out the actual statement, I was intimidated because I did not know if I really had that much to say about it. After writing what I had prepared to say, I was left to be honest and write what I was discovering about my work in that moment. Through the statement I was able to uncover an honesty in my writing and my painting simultaneously.

When looking at the body of work I have created this semester in English 1101, I view it much in the same way that I view the works of art I have created. Not only do I see the individual elements, but also the narrative told in its entirety. As I view a painting, I again face the feeling of the odds being against me to compete the piece. I can remember which portions I struggled to create, and the the exact stroke that I would consider the breakthrough of the composition. Once again, I experience the freedom when the piece has been resolved to its fullest potential and my work as the artist is complete. The portfolio I have composed for English 1101 is much like a single painting. I can remember which elements felt forced and unauthentic, the journey to resolve the issues, and the feeling of triumph as each piece became all it could be. The portfolio is a testament to what I can accomplish and highlights my growth as a writer.

Art: The Big, Bad Monster

Five grim faces set the tone for an advertisement addressing a heated topic for any young artist. One girl in a bright red shirt demands attention from the room by breaking up the dull figures and stagnant background. The bold, yellow type prepares the audience to take in a shocking statistic when really it reads, "1 in 5 teenagers will experiment with art." In the lower right hand corner, the ad encourages parents to "talk to [their] kids about art school." Upon first glance, one would never realize this is an advertisement for the College for Creative Studies. The ad was created in December of 2011 by the agency Team Detroit. Being one of many in an entire campaign, the ad was originally put up in poster format but gained popularity as the campaign began streaming through social media. The overall negative tone captures the problem many artists face today when considering school options. The ad brings a problem to the forefront, demanding the audience to consider the need to encourage young artists to pursue art despite the negative connotations society has given it.

When reading the conspicuous data presented in the advertisement, it is clear many view "experimenting with art" in a negative light. There is no logic to support the belief that art is negative, yet time and time again, artists are discouraged to pursue art as a career. On May 4, 2008, *emptyeasel.com* created an open poll asking, "As you were growing up, were you encouraged to be an artist? How did it affect your life choices?" Since the opening date of the poll, 270 people have participated. Of the 270, 81 said that "[they were] told to focus on other things, but [they] stuck with it anyway," and sadly, 64 said that "[they were] told to focus on other things, and [they] left art behind." After disregarding the 10% who had no interest in art at all, fewer than 60% of the people who answered the poll were encouraged to pursue hobbies other than art, or rather, suppress their desire to create art. The numbers speak for themselves; however, it is clear young artists are told art is not a suitable career path and a great deal of them are convinced of this notion. The vicious cycle of young artists abandoning their craft begins here, after being told "experimenting with art" is a negative thing. Team Detroit was aware of the trend to give up on making art and kept it in mind when creating the ad. There is nothing wrong with "experimenting with art." The ad is simply pointing out a phemonenon that clogs up young artists' opinions of their own passions, that art making is a discouraged practice. In an attempt to make young artists consider for themselves the practicality of art, the ad boldly throws out what society tells them: that "experimenting with art" results in nothing.

The ad is laid out in such a way that it grabs the emotions of the audience. The girl almost pushes her way to the mind of the reader not only because she is the only figure in a bright red shirt, but also because she looks as if she has something to hide. One can infer that she hides her passion for art because there is someone or something that puts artists in a negative light. The ad symbolizes this negativity by enclosing the girl in a sea of gray. Although she is surrounded by other teenagers, she seems cut off from them. Further emphasizing the themes of shame and isolation, the dull expressions on the teenagers' faces also convey a sense of negativity. It is easy to see that the images included in the ad play with the emotions of the viewer and activate a sense that the perusal of art is pointless. Who or what is creating the negative connotations when considering art? The ad itself gives one example as to who this could be by directing the information to a certain group. In the lower right hand corner, the ad says, "Talk to your kids about art school." It would seem as if the main audience the ad intends to reach out to is none other than the parents of the potential art students. By simply addressing parents, the ad indirectly labels them as one of the main threats to art's mutilated reputation. By including images that activate an emotional response and directing the information to the parents of young artists, the ad attempts to push specific viewers into a role of encouraging the pursuit of art rather than further hurting its reputation.

The ad points to another source creating negative art connotations by influencing the setting. Due to the multiple doors and books present in the background of the ad, it would seem the teenagers are in a school. The ad intentionally places them in this setting in order to point out school's negative influence on young artists. Sabrina Holcomb of the National Education Association writes that "arts education must fight for a seat in the classroom, despite the law's inclusion of the arts as a core academic subject." With everyone seemingly against them and consistently instilling the idea that art is not important enough to be included in the curriculum, how are future artists supposed to see their potential? It is not out of the question to presume many young artists choose to move past art in hopes of finding a more "suitable career." In fact, according to a "Teens and Careers survey" put on by Junior Achievement USA and ING, over the course of just one year, students saying they want a career in the arts after graduation dropped from 23% in 2012 to just 14% in 2013. It is clear that students coming out of high school are becoming more and more disinterested in the arts. The ad argues, by creating a visual of the girl being ostracized from her peers, that artists give up because they are shamed for having a passion for art. In making visual connections, the ad points to specific outside forces that contribute to the hurt many young artists face when considering artistic careers; this is done in order to inspire these forces to admit their habits of soiling art and instead learn to promote young artists.

When observing the ad, there is an obvious parallel to drug awareness posters. The ad mimics drug awareness posters' use of figures, feelings of being ostracized, and the commission to talk to the "lost teen" about his or her problem. Some viewers may take offense to the tactic used, but one must keep in mind the ad was not created to equate going to art school with the use of drugs; that would be nonsense and that is the point. The ad was created to allow young artists and their parents to carefully consider art school as an option. The parallel sets viewers up to consider the problem at hand with as much care as if their child was using drugs. At the same time, there is a hint of humor in the approach that serves to diffuse the issue as students and parents potentially talk about art school. The diffusion is created by rigidly emphasizing the big, bad monster art is made out to be. The informative nature of the ad gives it an importance that makes it nearly impossible to ignore. Since the issue raised is so often overlooked and dismissed, the importance created by the sarcastic nature of the ad is crucial. The parallel structure to many drug awareness posters is created intentionally so that the audience has no other option than to consider what the ad is saying about society — young artists are viewed as a disgrace and disappointment, when really their roles are vital.

Despite the opinions that dismiss art as having no importance, there is no doubt art is crucial to a flourishing society. In 1985, Arthur

Schlesinger, Jr., a professor of the humanities at the City University of New York, went against the traditional urge to dismiss art and instead emphasized how integral it is as a "public role" in society.Inhis piece, Schlesinger points out how foolish it is to believe that art is no less than "crucial to the forming of national traditions and to the preservation of civic cohesion." When looking at the ad, art and the desire to further one's knowledge in art is considered shameful and unnecessary. This idea could not be further from the truth. Often society tells young artists they need to suppress their desire to create, when really progress depends on forces of creativity. "National traditions" and "civic cohesion," being just as important as progress, call for a certain creativity as well. There is an endless need to move forward while still staying unified as a nation and holding to traditions. How can society accomplish such a complex task without creative minds? Just as Schlesinger points out the foolishness of modern belief in art, the ad works in the same way by spelling out what society believes so that it can hear and discover for itself how ridiculous the claim is. The ad counteracts the norms of society by poking fun at the illegitimacy of the negative connotations aimed toward art in hopes that young artists will not give up on their pursuits.

After considering all that encompasses the ad—the informative nature, the careful set up, the visuals, and the parallel structure—it is clear this ad was not just created to promote The College for Creative Studies. Had that been the goal, the ad would point out reasons why this art school is better than the rest. Team

Detroit noticed that there are not many people on the side of young artists, so they lead by example. The ad unapologetically points out the problem: artists are hindered by negative connotations. In hopes that they would recognize and change their habits, the ad refers to who is to blame for art's negative reputation: society, specifically parents and schools. The creators of the ad bring up these ideas so that young artists develop a sense of what they should do: carefully reconsider art school and the general pursuit of art. The real goal of this ad is to promote young artists and give them a voice to speak out against the norms of society.

Works Cited

"2013 Teens and Careers Survey." *JuniorAchievement USA*. ING, 2013. Web. 9 Sept. 2014.

Caridad, Paul. "Talk to Your Kids About Art." *Visual News*. N.p., 17 Feb. 2012. Web. 9 Sept. 2014.

Dan. "Were You Encouraged to Be an Artist?" *Empty Easel*. N.p., 9 May 2008. Web. 9 Sept. 2014.

Holcomb, Sabrina. "Arts Education." *neatoday.org*, National Education Association. 17 Jan. 2007. Web. 8 Sept. 2014.

Schlesinger, Arthur, Jr. "The Arts' Key Role in Our Society." *NYTimes.com*. The New York Times Company, 20 Sept. 1985. Web. 9 Sept. 2014.

Team Detroit. Advertisement. *sadanduseless.com*. Web. 2009. 9 Sept. 2014.

Art: Where Environment Meets Experience

During the 4th century B.C., Praxiteles became one of the first artists known for a work of art. When he created the sculpture *Aphrodite of Knidos*, it was not predominately viewed as propaganda or a means of celebrating ancient Greece, unlike the artwork that preceded it. *Aphrodite of Knidos* was commended and appreciated solely for its beauty rather than the fundamental techniques that were utilized to create it. Lovers of art during the 4th century B.C. swarmed to see it, even those from other parts of the world. Critics said, "Praxiteles [has] brought soul to marble" ("Praxiteles"). In modern days, lovers of art from all over the world still swarm to see *Aphrodite of Knidos* as they did in ancient times. Had the people in the 4th century B.C. not recognized the beauty of *Aphrodite of Knidos*, it might not have become as reputable despite its careful fabrication and uniqueness.

In the same way *Aphrodite of Knidos* engaged viewers through beauty and symbolism, modern day art not only serves various purposes in society but is also admired for what it represents and the pure beauty of it. Lovers of art can admire compositions by visiting galleries and museums. Particular galleries and museums receive more hype than others. For example, in Athens, Georgia, the gallery space in Hotel Indigo receives little attention as compared to the Georgia Museum of Art. Favorable art spaces shine a light on why certain works of art are more highly revered than others. Much like the renown of *Aphrodite of Knidos*, modern day artwork gains respect by people being willing to observe it. One role of gallery and museum spaces is to usher in a community to revere art. After having visited the gallery spaces in Hotel Indigo and the Georgia Museum of Art, it is clear to me that viewers' experiences in galleries and museums play a distinct role in their ability to appreciate the art.

Lovers of art and gallery-goers establish how art is perceived by the public and determine which forms are respected. Like any organization, art museums and galleries cater to their clientele. The images in these spaces should be selected because they are thought to evoke a sense of wonder and fascination among viewers inorder to draw them into the pieces. In hopes of learning how spaces dedicated to art influence the art community's reaction to certain compositions, I visited the Hotel Indigo gallery. Upon entering the hotel, the first thing I hear is a grown man asking the young, female worker at the front desk where the board room is located. He is wearing a polished, dark suit and appears to be flustered, making me think he is a business man running late for a meeting. After receiving his answer, I observe that his trek to the board room requires him to pass down the gallery hallway filled with local

artwork. Although he does not purposefully look at the art, his quick treads through the hallway soon lead him to the pinnacle gallery space in the hotel, a room dedicated to local works of art. He soon realizes the gallery space he has entered is the incorrect location and eventually finds his way to the less assuming board room. For a moment, I surmise that his initial reaction to enter the gallery space reveals how carefully considered it was when the hotel was being designed. It seems that the gallery space is thought to be more important than a room dedicated to business functions; however, the longer I sit in the space with no one coming to observe the artwork, the more I realize how detached the gallery really is from the happenings of the hotel. The gallery at Hotel Indigo lacks an ushering in of people from the art community, and more than that, outsiders of this community choose to ignore works of art even when they are forced upon them.

!Sitting in the lonely, concrete box that Hotel Indigo labels the art gallery, I consider my motives for observing this particular site. I had no intention of coming to this site. Originally, I wanted to visit the

Georgia Museum of Art; however, it is closed on Mondays as is the Lyndon House gallery, my second option. In a final effort, I chose to go to the Hotel Indigo gallery. It seems ironic that I sit in the gallery space upset that no one has yet come to appreciate the art when I, an artist, have ulterior motives for viewing it. In addition, I am uninspired to look at the art. It is almost like the disconnected nature of the gallery in relation to the hotel amenities creates a detached frame of mind when viewing the art. Hotel Indigo is an example of how "the premises or building… [has] an impact on how customers perceive the quality of exhibitions" (Pusa). The cold, resonant room coupled with its pushed aside orientation makes for a less than exciting experience at the gallery. As a viewer in the Hotel Indigo gallery, the disconnected orientation of the gallery causes an underwhelming experience that results in my opinion of the artwork to decline, thus demonstrating that the perception of art is influenced by the space in which it presides.

Viewers' experiences in a space dedicated to art are in part determined by their initial reaction upon entering the site. Immediately upon entering the Georgia Museum of Art, the environment comes alive as compared to Hotel Indigo. Before even being able to view a work of art, the museum has a front informational desk set up. I feel welcomed and can see that anyone would feel secure in knowing that there is a place dedicated to answering any questions he or she may have. The welcoming feeling I experience upon entering the Georgia Museum of Art is significantly different than that of the gallery in Hotel Indigo. Being the only one in the space, I felt as if I shouldn't have been there. The walls seemed to enclose me, and often I found myself avoiding the front deskso as to not be asked to leave. This was a completely irrational thought as it is a public gallery, but the lack of energy in the space led me to subconsciously feel that I did not belong there. In contrast, the lively scene and welcoming atmosphere I am now experiencing in the Georgia Museum of Art causes me to be in a better, more optimistic mood as I view the work. In addition, there is nothing distracting me, like avoiding the front desk in Hotel Indigo, from observing the art. My opinion of the compositions in the Georgia Museum of Art is superior as there is no negativity influencing my manner.

On the left, I observe a man being welcomed to the Georgia Museum of Art.
On the right, I avoid the front desk at Hotel Indigo by hiding in the narrow gallery hallway.

In order to ensure one's experience at an art gallery or museum space is positive, there is a need to engage all potential viewers. The Georgia Museum of Art successfully draws in a variety of people. I observe that the space is split up into two parts: contemporary galleries and historical galleries. Jamie Bull, an art professor at the University of Georgia, pointedly notes that "the museum has more space and more galleries. There is a lot more to see, pulling people from all over." In the Historical section of the museum, I am particularly intrigued by a certain man and young woman due to their vibrant discourse about the artwork on display. He is an older gentleman dressed appropriately for the outing in a collared shirt and khaki pants. In contrast, the young woman, who seems to be his daughter or pupil, lacks the gentility of the man as she is dressed in jeans and a t-shirt. He points to the art saying, "Do you see this?" She responds in a quiet tone. Again he enthusiastically says, "Look at it!" From his thought-out wardrobe to his emotion when viewing the compositions, the artwork from the historical section of the museum seems to appeal more to the older gentleman than it does to the

young woman. I observe another pair consisting of a young man and woman who both appear to be students. Much of the Georgia Museum of Art's success comes from the student body at the University of Georgia as "a lot of their exhibits are set up for education purposes" (Jamie Bull). The museum specifically is a great resource for students who "are studying Art History to be able to see concrete examples" (Jamie Bull). The students I am observing, however, are in the contemporary section of the museum. They engage in plain dialogue, which seems less in depth as compared to the first pair due to their periodic giggling and fast pace as they move from piece to piece. It seems that certain age groups are drawn to different types of artwork and react to them in different ways. The older gentleman seems to prefer the historical artwork while the younger students seem to prefer the contemporary artwork. I notice that the compositions in the Hotel Indigo gallery have a "contemporary, very in the now" style, much like the artwork that the students in the Georgia Museum of Art responded to the most (Jamie Bull). Jamie Bull, having had pieces in Hotel Indigo, questions if the gallery "draws in the everyday person." It is plausible that the art is ignored in Hotel Indigo because the contemporary works do not artistically cater to the needs of the professional business environment. The Georgia Museum of Art, being aware of their vast scope of clientele, selects works of art that engage all age groups, causing viewers' perception of the compositions to be heightened.

The space in which a work of art presides influences the viewer's experience and perception of the piece. *Aphrodite of Knidos*, for example, was located in the temple of Aphrodite Euploia. According to Lucian in his work *Amores*, "The temple had a door on both sides for the benefit of those also who wish to have a good view of the goddess from behind so that no part of her be left unadmired." The environment in which *Aphrodite of Knidos* was located allowed for a full-on experience, therefore influencing the way people admired and perceived her. The temple had a respect for the statue, encouraging viewers to revere every angle of it. In the same way, modern day museums and galleries create a context for which the pieces inside are viewed. The Georgia Museum of Art creates a better atmosphere for viewing art than the Hotel Indigo gallery because the layout serves to welcome the viewer and it address every type of person who may observe the pieces inside. Because the environment allows for a better frame of mind when viewing the artwork, the compositions in the Georgia Museum of Art may be determined by the art community to be more significant and all around more successful. As art is a subjective matter, it is important that every aspect of one's experience with the piece is addressed. The art community cannot assume the artists who created the compositions in Hotel Indigo are less skilled than those who created the pieces in the Georgia Museum of Art; they can, however, only glean from a piece that which the environment allows for. Thus, the environment in which a composition resides determines how interactive and fulfilling the work of art is to the viewer.

Works Cited

Aphrodite of Knidos. 2008. 360-330 B.C. Vatican Museum. flik .com. F. Tronchin, 22 March 2008. Web. 24 Oct. 2014. Photograph posted to photo sharing website.

Bull, Jamie. Personal Interview. 21 October 2014.

"Praxiteles." ancientgreece.com. University Press Inc., 2003-2012. Web. 17 Oct. 2014.

"Pseudo-Lucian: Affairs of the Heart." Amores. Trans. A.M. Harmon.well. com. The Well Group, Inc., 2001. Web. 23 Oct. 2014.

Pusa, Sofia, and Lisa Uusital . "Creating Brand Identity in Art Museums: A Case Study." *International Journal of Arts Management* 17.1 (2014): 18-24. *Business Source Complete*. Web. 13 October 2014.

Shrewsbury, Alyssa. Compare and Contrast Georgia Museum of Art and the Hotel Indigo Gallery. 2014. JPEG fil .

Shrewsbury, Alyssa. Georgia Museum of Art. 2014. Photograph.

Shrewsbury, Alyssa. Hotel Indigo Gallery. 2014. Photograph.

The Art of Revision

Although there is not one way to go about a painting, my art teacher encourages the class to follow an order to make sure the entire piece develops to its full potential. When painting a still life, we are first instructed to quickly pencil out the section we choose to do. We are then told to take out our biggest brush and paint large blocks of color, making sure we address our darkest darks and lightest lights. The majority of the time is dedicated to developing the blocks of color so that they eventually take shape into recognizable objects. The final step is to take out a small brush and paint in the small details and fix any area that lost its form during the process.

These four steps, penciling out, blocks of color, taking shape, and refining encompass my revision process when writing. Below is a portion of my Biography that serves as an example of how I incorporate the four revision steps.

Key: Changes made are marked in blue.

Penciling Out

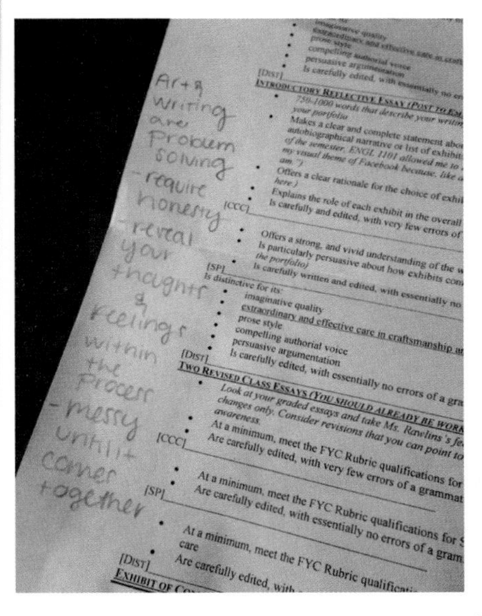

Art and Writing are problem solving
-require honesty
-reveal your thoughts and feelings within the process
- messy until it comes together

Above I included an image of my original notes that I made at the time of inspiration. Beside the image I have written out what the notes say. As shown, the penciling out portion of the process is very minimal. My art teacher says that when penciling out a drawing that is intended to be painted, it is important to make the objects of the still life smaller than they actually appear in order to leave room on the page to expand once it is time to paint the image. In the same way, I have kept my ideas very basic so that further along in the writing process, I have room to expand upon my ideas without being hindered.

Blocks of Color:

Art being a way to express one's feelings has an element of honesty. Writing comes from the same place. Both are different forms of

As I create a work of art, I try not to have a finished product in mind as to allow the piece to develop in organically. An important element in impactful writing is for some of the connections to be made in the moment as the work is coming together. In doing this, one's thoughts and feelings toward the subject develop in a natural way.

creating a work of art is often a messy process. The hectic element of the composition, although not pleasant in the moment, adds to the development of the piece as a whole, creating a redemptive sense when the work is complete. In the same way, the writing process may be messy, but is necessary for a completely authentic and thought out piece. When the work is complete, the writer will see not see the finished product, but elements of working out the piece.

At this point in the writing process, I have brainstormed, addressing each topic I mentioned in the outline. My ideas are expanding, but they are separate from one another and remain unfinished. The paragraph is a bit choppy,

but like my art teacher says, it is important to address the entire piece before developing the individual parts.

Taking Shape

Elements in art and writing coincide as they both allow the creator to display outwardly a subject being worked out inwardly. Because of the expressive nature of both art and writing, a sense of honesty is the result. In order to be fully honest in these two acts, the creator must show genuine thought process by making connections during the process and allowing the piece to develop organically. For both an artist and a writer, it is important to not have a finished product in mind as to allow the piece to develop in a natural way. Often, this will create for a messy process while elements of the piece, whether art or writing, are not fully established. The hectic element of the composition, although not pleasant in the moment, adds to the development of the piece as a whole, creating a redemptive sense when the work is complete. When the work is complete, the creator will see not only the finished product, but elements of working out the problem, making for a completely authentic and thought out piece.

Whereas before the ideas were very much separated from each other, the paragraph is starting to make sense together. In order to establish unity, I had to change around the order of some of the phrases I wanted to include from the previous

step. The context and flow I have inserted around my claims introduce evidence and development to the paragraph. I have also created an introduction and conclusion that reference the same idea (which I have highlighted in orange) in order to increase cohesion. In terms of painting, the image is taking shape and is beginning to work together. Now, the viewer can recognize the objects (the ideas) and appreciate the entire image (the entire paragraph) as a whole.

Refining

Elements of art and writing coincide as they both allow the creator to display outwardly a subject being worked out inwardly. Because of the expressive nature of both art and writing, a sense of honesty is the result. In order to be fully honest in these two crafts, the creator must show a genuine thought process by making connections during the process and allowing the piece to develop organically. For both an artist and a writer, it is important to not have a finished product in mind as to allow the piece to develop in a natural way. Often, this will create for a messy process while elements of the piece, whether art or writing, are not fully established. The hectic sense of the composition, although not pleasant in the moment, adds to the development of the piece as a whole, creating for a redemptive element when the work is complete. Looking back on the project, the creator will see not only the finished product, but reminders of working out the problem, making for a completely authentic and thought out piece.

At this point in the revision process, I have gone into the paragraph and made some minor changes. My art teacher always says that toward the end of the painting process, it is important to touch up certain areas where the paint may have gotten muddied as more and more was added to the piece. Some of my word choices, seeming to make sense earlier on in the process, may no longer make fit in with the paragraph and need to be changed. For instance, in the last sentence, I changed the word "elements" to "reminders" not only because I felt the word better captured the idea, but also because "elements" is used in many other places throughout the paragraph. By making appropriate word and transition changes, I work toward increasing coherence.

Using the four revision steps, I can be sure that my ideas develop at a consistent rate. By starting off writing in a simple format and building up, my development of the topic is genuine and not bounded by what has already been written. The process ensures that certain parts of the paragraph are not forgotten and all is addressed equally. By following the revision steps, my papers can reach their fullest potential.

The Art of the Peer Review

Often I find that when I am struggling to draw something accurately, I need someone else to tell me the areas of my drawing that are problematic. After receiving another's advice, I am able to refine whatever it is I am attempting to draw. When creating an entire composition, it is tempting to focus in on a single area and lose sight of the piece as a whole. While it is important that the quality of the individual components of a composition are up to par, the effect of them working together make for a far more impactful piece. Others' perspectives also aid in this situation as they are able to view the entirety of a piece for what it is and not for what it is supposed to be.

In the same way, the writing process can become very confused and complicated. Often, writers read their work in light of what they feel it should accomplish when in reality it falls short of their goal. There is often a need to receive someone else's perspective in order to make sense of the writing. The peer reviewing process allows for a much needed fresh perspective on one's work.

Below, I have inserted a portion of a peer review that I created for Sarah Grace. As her peer review partner, it is my goal to help Sarah Grace not lose sight of her entire essay as a whole. I do this by incorporating grammar and wording changes within the paragraph and adding comments to the end of each paragraph in order to help her see how successful it is in supporting her thesis. The end comments also include what I felt the paragraph accomplished in terms of the prompt assigned. By including this information, Sarah

Grace is encouraged to consider the unity and development of her topic from paragraph to paragraph. I feel that by approaching the peer review in this way, I am able to help Sara Grace consider not only the individual aspects of her essay but also the work in its entirety.

Key:
Parts of essay being revised
My comments within the paragraph
My end comments

Audience Paragraph:

I created a calendar for an audience that is still eligible to participate in Freshman College. Add in the word "community" after "college". Many only see the side of schoolwork and two hour and fifteen minute classes. Confusing sentence - maybe say, "Many students going in to college are only aware of the academic side of their futures." Yes, that sounds like a miserable way to spend your last summer before heading off to college, but there are people there to I think you mean "who" instead of "to". get you through every minute of every class, no comma necessary and through every minute of the times you don't need this not spent in class.

Great job defining a clear audience! Make your final sentence connects back to your thesis in order to increase coherence.

How Paragraph:

Creating a calendar maximized Change "maximize" to "maximizes". Try to write in present tense when you can. the opportunities to show the bonds created and kept over time. Using a Microsoft calendar template for each month from July to October, I put in specific events and pictures that participants in Freshman College (instead say: "the Freshman College community") did together and took that created (instead say: "that resulted in") growth within their society. For example in the Month of July 16 , I put in the events that we were required to do, like the ropes course, the rafting trip, and our field day, to show activities that required team work to get through. To avoid say "require" twice in the same sentence, try saying, "to show activities that use teamwork to be completed." I then included a picture from the rafting trip and from another activity we had to do called "Brush a Bulldawg". In the photo from the rafting trip 20, you can see the connection of the two girls standing in the front made from conquering rafting down the river together.

Awesome paragraph! I could clearly understand what you did even without viewing the images. Again, just connect your last sentence of your paragraph back to the thesis. This will make the artist statement more coherent.

Passion and Purpose

I know there is something radical inside of all of us. There is a passion and purpose for everyone that is waiting to be found. This belief of mine is the inspiration for my piece. Despite the purpose I believe is in all, I see many people living the life of a dead man because they are dead to their passions. I want to draw attention to this tragedy though my passion: art. My intent is that this piece would act as a force, pushing people toward a hunger for purpose in such a way that when viewing my art, people would see themselves and would be moved to make a change in their lives. Through specific techniques and design choices in my piece, I hope to shine a light on the sad reality of how people do not apply themselves to their passions; in doing so, I allow room for change.

It is not the individual elements of my painting but how the elements work together that convey my idea. The piece is a minimal image, composed on an elongated strip of fabric cut into four sections, the topmost being the largest. Six goldfish are the subject matter, which primarily reside on the bottom half of the fabric. With such a simple image, the viewer can rest assured that every detail of the composition was considered and has an integral function in the piece as a whole. One may ask, "What do goldfish have to do with passion and purpose?" I chose to use goldfish as the subject matter because despite the scientific truth, as a child I remember equating goldfish to having a short attention span. The idea of distraction plays

a role in why people do not go after what they are passionate about. As the fabric on which the image is painted is split up into four sections, there are four distinguishable characteristics of society I want to draw attention to. The first, bottom-most section relates to the reality in which people currently live. I purposefully made this secti

grime of reality in which we choose to reside. The second section represents modern day goals. This section is purposefully small because people only allow themselves to go so far in terms of reaching goals. Society allows so much to hinder people from achieving more. The third section represents our dreams and desires. Again, this section is purposefully small because society puts a filter on how far dreams and desires can go. Because society only lives in a small portion of reality, does not reach for higher goals, and only allows dreams to be so big, rarely do people tap into their passions, making them all that they could be: people filled with purpose. The infinite realm of a person with purpose is represented by the fourth, largest section of the piece. Here, the goldfish seem more dispersed, as there are few people who find and live out a life of passion. My hope is that as people view this image, they ponder their own lives and evaluate if they are taking part in an infinitely full life or have taken their place among the grime of reality.

My ideas do not come across at first glance when viewing the piece as they are heavily dependent on symbolism. This, however, is done purposefully in order to reach a wider audience. I specifically want to reach the younger generation who have a least an appreciation for art. Since my audience is not specifically the artist community, I did not want to create an image that would be daunting or intimidating to look at if the viewer does not consider himself or herself an artist. I wanted to create an image that relates to everyone who views it and is not too much to take in. With such an important theme behind it, I wanted the image to be approachable so that the viewer would consider the call to action. As my audience is a younger generation, perhaps students in high school and college, I feel that one of the best modes for the piece would be the Internet. By photographing and uploading the image on Facebook and other social media sites, my desired audience can be reached. Photographing the painting would also allow it to be viewed in the way it was designed to be viewed. The piece, being made of fabric, allows light to shine through when placed in front of a window. It is specifically designed to hang in front of a window that takes up half of the wall. This way, it is only the fish that exist in the upper regions that are glowing and shedding light into the room in which that piece resides. For me as the artist, it is important that the entire experience rather than just the image itself be considered when viewing the piece. Light, being an outside element, becomes one of the most important and intriguing parts of the piece. By lighting up the fish in the upper region, the viewer notices something different about them and is drawn to them. By tailoring my ideas around the audience and the orientation of the piece, the viewers are encouraged to consider the call to live a life of passion and purpose.

My purpose in making the painting is to help create an atmosphere for people to consider for themselves if they are doing or are poising themselves to do what they are passionate about. I felt that there was no better way to convey this idea than through my passion for art. For me, art is such a powerful tool because under any circumstance it has a use, even if it is for the artist who created it alone. I know that, for some viewers, the meaning of my piece is going to fly over their heads as the symbolism may be difficult to interpret without an explanation. For some, all my piece will be is a painting of goldfish. Even in this situation, my piece still serves an important purpose for me. When I look at the image, I am reminded of the journey it took to create a piece that depicted something that was important to me. I am reminded of my passion and how important it is to continue using it to shine a light on others. Even if I am the only person who gleans anything from the piece, it served its purpose in pushing someone closer to the person the world needs them to be.

English 1102

Student: Lauren Rich

Lauren Rich uses the metaphor of cave exploration to unify her ePortfolio. While students often choose a hobby or passion as a portfolio theme, Lauren's "spelunking" is strictly figurative. She might not spend time in actual caves, but for her, both the process of finding her "niche" at UGA and developing as a writer could feel a great deal like the scary-but-rich experience of cave exploration.

A Lesson in the Art of Spelunking

"Life is 10% situation and 90% perception. You have to create your own happiness." I stared into the faces of 300 soon-to-be high school graduates. My speech was coming to an end. Only a few more sentences and a final farewell before we would all go our separate ways. I had practiced countless times, but I never expected what came next. Tears, regret, longing. Where had the last four years gone? Why were so many faces in the crowd still complete strangers? How could I say goodbye when I never said hello? I felt my throat well as a sob threatened to escape into the microphone and across the auditorium. I took a breath and continued, my voice like a dew drop hanging from a leaf, quivering and threatening to break away at any moment. "So, class of 2014, thank you for everything. I wish you so much more than luck."

My name is Lauren Rich. University of Georgia freshman, humankind aficionado, and avid spelunker. These are two truths and a sort-of lie. I don't "spelunk" in the strictest terms. In fact, I have never been in a literal cave. Instead, I spend many of my days exploring the vast grotto called introversion. I enjoy examining the stalactites of missed opportunities and the deep crevices of unrealized potential. Along the way, I sometimes see vast waterfalls of would-be friendships and the occasional "maybe tomorrow" stalagmite. Although these sites are certainly beautiful in their own way, I have been circling in the dark for too long, and what I crave now more than anything is sunlight.

Following the aforementioned graduation speech when I realized how much of my high school years were wasted on nervousness and procrastination, I vowed to change. No longer would I be the timid, quiet one who stuttered her name and only found solace surrounded by the lined paper of a journal. In Athens, I would be more forward, more involved, more amiable. I certainly did not expect to stand out among the other 34,999 students, but I did expect to find a niche in which I would spread my wings and flourish like never before. But, the heat of the summer brought with it complacency. By the time I arrived at the University of Georgia, I was just as withdrawn and future-oriented as ever. I kept to myself and my high school acquaintances, giving hardly a thought to the enormous amount of opportunity that surrounded me. There I was, trudging away through introversion, trying to find the smallest promise of an exit. My new beginning quickly turned into a continuation of the life I swore against just six months before.

But, I will admit that this is a very negative view of a very positive situation. I am *only* four months into the best years of my life thus far. Though I have traveled deep into the recesses of quiet acceptance and dissatisfaction, I have with me both flashlight and map. Self-improvement has no deadline, and August 12, 2014 was certainly not my final opportunity to escape this introversion rut. So, now that you have an idea of who I am, allow me to say who I strive to be. The unparalleled scholar Dr. Seuss once wrote, "Today I will behave as if this is the day I will be remembered." Today, I will strive to escape this formidable cave of isolation, to bask in the sunlight, to brave the untouched waters of sociability, to be remembered.

Caving How-To

Finding the Right Location

When I first entered this English 1102 class, I could not help but feel a tinge of resentment. Despite all of my hard work in high school and my love for literature, I still could not manage a "5" on either AP Literature or AP Language exams. So there I sat, hearing that illusory "5" laughing in the distance as I scowled at the coming semester. At the first mention of a portfolio, a documented chronology of my "composition journey," I felt uneasy. I already felt well-established in my composition skills and did not expect this course to offer much help.

Now at the conclusion of this semester, I am happy to retract my previous sentiments and denounce the conceited attitude that brought me to them in the first place. As a result of this course, I have improved in both composition and character. I no longer struggle to accept constructive peer criticism, and I now view English 1102 not as a punishment for my inability to score a "5," but as a valuable means to improvement.

Gathering Equipment

For my first essay, I chose to analyze one of my favorite short stories, Joyce Carol Oates's "Where Are You Going, Where Have You Been?" I knew that I wanted to explore Oates's comments on childhood expectations versus the realities of adulthood. However, my first draft showed only simple character analyses of Connie and Arnold Friend and a lack of a contentious thesis. I stated that Connie represents "the stereotypical rebellious teen who longs for an idealized sense of independence, yet does not understand what true independence entails" and Arnold Friend is "everything Connie hopes to attain" (Paper 1). Though the text supports both characterizations, my first draft does not offer a substantial analysis of the short story or Oates's controversial assertions, and in the conclusion, I introduced an entirely new topic of obedience and Oates's "warning of the dangers of hedonism" (Paper 1). Even in my second draft, I held tight to this flimsy assertion. Thankfully, I revisited my conclusion in my final draft. Instead of considering "Where Are You Going" as just a cautionary tale, I asserted that Oates "relay[s] a time-worn lesson concerning the tragic permanence of lost innocence" (Paper 1). Though my final draft was far from perfect, I could already see improvement in my thought process.

Wandering the Cave

After completing Paper 1, I realized the greatest need for Paper 2 was a debatable, and perhaps even contentious, thesis. I wanted to challenge myself with a truly factious argument. Therefore, I decided to focus on John Updike's criticism of 1950s America in his short story "A&P." I asserted that the author uses his narrator's escape from the monotonous A&P as a means to support the emerging counterculture youth movement, particularly the Beat Generation.

In my first draft, the entirety of my research seemed to lie in the introductory paragraph, which made for an overwhelming introduction. There, I described the ideals of the "Fabulous Fifties," the dissatisfaction of many youths, and the basic pillars of the Beats. By doing this, I made it difficult for my readers to truly understand what the counterculture movement entailed, which would impede the clarity of my argument. So, I added a paragraph to my second draft describing the Beats and giving examples of Beat literature to further illustrate their "separation from the norm" (Paper 2). However, this paragraph did not thoroughly relate back to my thesis.

My main focus for both my third and final drafts was explicitly stating the relationship between the details I chose to include and my thesis. For example, in my second body paragraph of the final draft, I cited Allen Ginsberg's poem "America" to illustrate the Beat condition. Instead of simply including quotes or sparse analysis of the poem itself, as I did in previous drafts, I explained what the poem revealed about Beat culture and how Updike expounds on these characteristics in "A&P." I would like to believe that this Paper 2 is my best writing and my most effective argument of the semester.

Relying on Other Explorers

Perhaps my greatest struggle in this course was the peer review process. As I stated before, I was initially skeptical of peer criticism. It would concern me to see how many comments a reviewer might have for parts of my essay I thought were well constructed. It was not until Paper 2 that I truly saw the merits of peer review.

My review partners for Paper 2 were more than helpful with their suggestions. For example, one reviewer suggested that my analysis of Ginsberg's poetry was interesting, but it was "unclear what these pieces [had] to do with Updike's statement" (Review 2). Similarly, the same reviewer challenged me to strengthen my analysis and connections in certain paragraphs by stating that "[they lack] the depth that you need. Think about asking why a little bit more. Why [do] these quotes matter? And what [do] they do for the piece and the point you are trying to make?" (Review 2).

I can definitely see notable changes in my view of criticism. Instead of an unwelcome nuisance, I now view peer review as a valuable way to gain insight into my composition style. This review process has illuminated shortcomings and strategies for improvement, and I am thankful for both.

Exploring on My Own

For my Wild Card, I wanted to show my thoughts at their most basic. I included several unedited monologues that I wrote while employing a creative "blind writing" exercise. The first describes an ongoing internal "video" that played through my head of a malleable ball rolling down a large staircase, the second expresses a longing for childish play, and the third portrays my thoughts on dissatisfaction and passion. There is no central theme for these writing samples. Instead, they are like fragments of my internal monologue on different days, always changing and always strange.

Lauren Rich
Raffaela Wilson
ENGL 1102
18 September 2014

"Where Are You Going, Where Have You Been?": Delusions versus Reality

Joyce Carol Oates's short story "Where Are You Going, Where Have You Been?" offers a sinister look at an egotistic adolescent's search for freedom and its aversive consequences. Teenaged Connie spends her nights pursuing the fruits of independence while giving no thought to its labors until the illusory Arnold Friend offers her that which she desires most. The luxurious and carefree lifestyle she expects to accompany adulthood lies in stark contrast to the mysterious and frightening world Friend propositions. Through extensive symbolism and characterizations, Oates explores the age-old topic of independence and presents a vivid illustration of childish delusions versus the realities of adulthood.

Connie serves as the stereotypical rebellious teen who longs for an idealized sense of freedom, yet she fails to realize that her desire for independence is rooted in fantasy. She is a young and immature fifteen and yet presents herself as an experienced adult. To mask her childishness, she nurtures two personas: a disinterested teen for family and a glimmering sensualist for friends and strangers. Her nights "across the highway" suggest that Connie frequently escapes the tedium of home and deviates into hedonism, where she entertains herself with older friends, strange boys, and "what haven and what blessing [she] yearned for" (1409). On these nights, Connie flaunts her sexualized self, symbolized by her "pullover jersey blouse that looked one way when she was at home and another way when she was away from home" (1408). Her unwillingness to establish a permanent "self" shows not only confusion, but also a childish obstinacy that betrays the mask she wears "anywhere that was not home" (1408).

As Oates describes her, Connie appears to be entirely fixated on the superficial and convinced that an adult semblance is equitable to maturity. She admits that "she was pretty, and that was everything," and even suspects that the strength of her mother's love is contingent upon beauty, remarking that her mother "preferred [Connie] to [sister] June, because she was prettier" (1408, 1410). By including this fixation, Oates presents Connie as a flippant child who mistakes the face for the mind. If nothing else, her ideals concerning beauty prove that Connie is plagued by the immaturity she so desperately tries to hide. Connie's ignorance cannot remain hidden under her thin veil of deception. The reader finds that, despite her objections, Connie has yet to establish an appreciation for true autonomy. Oates implies that Connie's nightly excursions are short-lived (she only spends three hours with a boy on the particular night Oates describes) and her family has remained a beacon of safety. No matter how far away she ventures, home always waits for her at the end of whatever alley she explores. Though she would never admit it, Connie is still totally dependent on the safety her family provides.

In her search for carte blanche, Connie attracts the strange Arnold Friend, who comes to represent everything Connie hopes to attain in adulthood. As his name foreshadows, Friend treats his and Connie's young relationship with unwarranted intimacy. His first comment to her is an alarming "Gonna get you, baby," and when he later arrives at her home unannounced, he offers to drive her away before even revealing his name (1409). This audacity coupled with an aura of mystery establishes Arnold Friend as the embodiment of Connie's desires, namely freedom. Friend's ostentatious "convertible jalopy painted gold," complete with his name inscribed on the side, and a crude portrait of himself, symbolizes Friend's enticing independence (1409). Unlike Connie, Arnold Friend is not bound by watchful family members or adult chauffeurs. Connie notes this nomadic spirit when she remarks that "he had driven up the driveway all right but had come from nowhere before that and belonged nowhere" (1415). It is this characteristic that entrances Connie, leading her unknowingly to her ruination.

In addition to his freedom (of which Connie is certainly envious), Friend portrays himself as the perfect and normal rebellious youth. He dresses stylishly ("the way all of them dressed") and appears to have all of the desirable attributes of the time (1412). However, under the guise of the stereotype lies something sinister. Connie recognizes the familiarity of Friend's motions, such as his "sleepy, dreamy smile . . . the singsong way he talked . . . the way he tapped one fist against the other," yet she admits that "these things did not come together"(1414). She remarks that "his whole face was a mask" and suggests several times that his hair resembled a wig (1416). Following these accusations, Connie observes Friend's difficulty walking, noting that "his feet did not go all the way down; his boots must have been stuffed with something" (1417). Along with physical dissonance, Friend layers outdated colloquialisms, as though he is "no longer sure which one of them was in style" (1418). He claims that he "[knows] everybody" and tells Connie that she has been marked with his sign: "an X in the air" (1413, 1414). This observation in particular suggests that Arnold Friend not only represents a beastly immorality, he represents the literal "Beast" himself. Friend's difficulty walking implies cloven hooves and his misuse of youthful phrases characterizes him as a calculating predator versed in aggressive mimicry. Like a mockingjay, he uses familiar calls to trick and ensnare his victims. He wears an attractive mask to exploit Connie's ignorance, and, once the mask is removed, escape is impossible.

Just as Connie fails to see any of the negative aspects of adulthood, she is slow to realize Friend's devious intentions. Friend is the embodiment of carnality and presents Connie with everything she desires: freedom, sex, and adventure. It is not until Friend loses his charming facade that Connie understands the danger that confronts her. When he tells Connie, "I'm your lover" and promises her, "I'll hold you so tight you won't think you have to try to get away . . . because you'll know you can't," Connie finally recognizes Friend as an enemy (1416). In her desperation, she reaches out to figures of authority. Realizing that she has lost control, Connie threatens to call the police and insists that her father will soon come home (1416). These cries for help mark the beginning of Connie's regression into infancy. Severed from the familiarity of family and home, Connie abandons her glossy veneer and, at the climax of her transformation, "[cries] for her mother" over the telephone (1418). Despite Connie's anguish, Friend still forces upon her the life she once desired, thus uprooting Connie from youth and propelling her into the alien lands of adulthood.

"Where Are You Going, Where Have You Been?" reveals the schism between dreams and the waking world. The daunting realm Arnold Friend presents to young Connie destroys her tragically rosy view of adulthood. Without her family as a safety net, Connie reconsiders her search for independence and, in her struggle against the evil personified by Arnold Friend, realizes the precious transience of youth. When Connie remarks that she "did not recognize [any land] except to know that she was going to it," Oates uses this detail to relay a time-worn lesson concerning the tragic permanence of lost innocence.

Works Cited

Oates, Joyce Carol. "Where Are You Going, Where Have You Been?" *Making Literature Matter:* An Anthology for Readers and Writers. Ed. John Clifford and John Schilb. Boston: Bedford/St. Martin's, 2012. 1408-1420. Print.

Lauren Rich

Raffaela Wilson

ENGL 1102

4 December 2014

"A&P" and the Beat Generation

1960s America presented the country with a myriad of social and economic changes. Within a short decade, the Civil Rights Movement gained momentum, Cold War tensions remained heated, and leaders continued to push a war steadily losing public approval. With a change in culture and attitude came a change in people. Perhaps most notable was the rise of the Beat Generation, which spawned the counterculture revolution. In his short story "A&P," John Updike uses an allegorical tale to support the "beatniks" and to challenge the social confinement so prevalent following World War II. To illustrate the author's progressive opinion of the new youth movement, Updike's narrator escapes the banal A&P, a journey symbolizing his transition from the "Lost Generation" of World War II to a movement raw and unparalleled.

The Beats found their beginnings in the 1950s, during which the economy boomed and the nation enjoyed a brief period of peace epitomized by the stereotypical Fabulous Fifties. However, not everyone was content with this new age of consumerism and the facade of the *Leave It to Beaver* household. As Clark Dougan and Samuel Lipsman explain in *A Nation Divided*, many Americans found fault in this new wave of collective mindset. They believed the country valued social norms over individuality and financial gain over spiritual enlightenment (Dougan and Lipsman 34). An unrivaled youth subculture bloomed in the 1960s, rooted in nonconformity and watered with rock-n-roll beats and the bop of new, energizing literature (Dougan and Lipsman 35). The aptly-named Silent Generation of the previous decades quietly withered away to make room for its much more colorful counterparts who would eventually become known as the "Beats" (Dougan and Lipsman 34).

Completely disenchanted with American society, the Beats initially emerged as a low-profile movement that encouraged "rebellion against prevailing cultural standards" (Dougan and Lipsman 34). The Beats pursued this separation from convention mainly through subversive literature. Poet Allen Ginsberg, one of the Beat movement's most prominent figures, offered a testimony of the Beat condition in his 1956 poem "America." In "America," Ginsberg denounces the country's hypocrisy and advocates subversion and rebellion, characteristics of the Beats that Updike promotes in "A&P." Using direct, sometimes explicit statements, such as "Go fuck yourself with your atom bomb," and "America I am the Scottsboro boys," Ginsberg reveals his desire to disconnect from the country he so fervently condemns (5, 33). As John Clellon Holmes reveals in his editorial "This Is The Beat Generation," the Beats sought more than anything a separation from bravado and "a sort of nakedness of mind, and, ultimately, of soul" (10). At the core of almost all Beat literature lies this search for rebellion. Blatant discussions of dissatisfaction and sedition rocked the foundation of American society. Perhaps incited by the Beats, John Updike includes characters in "A&P" that show a similar desire to escape the authoritarianism and stagnation of tradition.

To illustrate the growing battle between the conventional and the avant-garde, John Updike uses his setting and characters as symbols of the developing social unrest. The A&P supermarket, with its structured atmosphere and knack for conformity, represents the suburban psyche of 1950s America. A supermarket of any kind serves as the heart of a community—the place into which every citizen must inevitably venture. Therefore, this hub is representative of the people who frequently visit. Updike's observant narrator Sammy is quick to establish his local A&P as one of hopeless tedium and structure. He characterizes his customers as "sheep," "houseslaves in pin curlers," and "scared pigs in a chute" (616, 618). Each of these derisive terms evokes a sense of conformity and captivity. The A&P-ers have evidently become lost in suburbia as they amble through the familiar store, or, if taken symbolically, the tedium of Americana. The scathing tone with which Sammy describes his environment both foreshadows his decision to leave and illustrates Updike's opposition to traditional American society.

Just as the A&P represents the cookie-cutter 1950s America, the three bikini-clad girls who upset the status quo represent the counter-culture Beats that gained popularity in the following decade. As early as the first line, Updike draws parallels between the trio and this new social insurrection. "A&P" begins with an abrupt fragment, as though the narrator was busy telling his story and the reader only started listening during the most interesting part. "In walk three girls in nothing but bathing suits," he reminisces (614). This brusque introduction describes both the girls' surprising entrance and that of the counterculture movement, which seemed to emerge as a colorful splash against a plain white canvas. When Sammy describes the leader of the girls, affectionately dubbed "Queenie," he dwells on her bare shoulders, neck, and wrists (617). He gawks at the idea that "there was nothing between the top of the suit and the top of her head except just *her*" and that her empty hands were "bare as God made them" (615, 617). This exposure is not just one of the body, but one of the spirit—the girls have sloughed away any excess, leaving only their natural selves. Updike perhaps incorporates this detail to draw further similarities between the Beats and the girls. With her exposed shoulders and stomach, Queenie exhibits the nakedness and bohemianism that became synonymous with "Beat."

Updike further explores the innate differences between Queenie and the other characters when he comments on their socioeconomic disparities. The narrator points to Queenie's purchase of "Kingfish Fancy Herring Snacks in Pure Sour Cream: 49¢" as an indication of her financial superiority (617). He then imagines her glamorous family gatherings and compares her "drinks the color of water with olives and sprigs of mint in them" with his much less sophisticated "Schlitz in tall glasses with 'They'll Do It Every Time' stenciled on" (617). Perhaps Updike incorporates this schism not to bring attention to the characters' socioeconomic inequality, but rather as a symbol of their differences in states of being. Queenie seems to be in a much different, much more ideal place than the narrator. She is unencumbered by social customs or the demoralizing stares of the sheep. It is for this reason that Sammy decides to follow her out of the harsh fluorescence of the A&P into Queenie's world where "sunshine is skating around on the asphalt" (619). The positive way in which Updike portrays Sammy's escape from the A&P illustrates the author's liberal view of nonconformity. Ignoring Lengel's reproval, the narrator continues his denial of the establishment and solidifies his desire to join the trio and thus the new youth movement.

In addition to the A&P itself, the store authority, Lengel, also embodies the atmosphere of the Fabulous Fifties. He serves as the voice of normalcy and tradition when he reprimands the three scantily-clad girls. This admonition reveals a character trait most representative of the era: an aversion to change. When faced with opposition from the trio of girls, the store's patrons succumb to fear, much like the proponents of tradition confronted by the Beats. Once the girls upset the natural order of the store, the other customers gathered together to avoid the scene like livestock herded by dogs. Lengel gives a voice to the petrified sheep when he cites decent dress and store policy to discourage the store's invaders (618). Following this argumentative scene, Sammy abruptly quits his job and chases after the girls, indicating his decision to abandon the conventions of the era and pursue uncharted territory. By recognizing the pitiful state of the A&P and subsequently deciding to quit his job, Sammy actually acknowledges the store and Lengel as representations of a weary and jaded country.

In "A&P," John Updike illustrates the birth of the Beat Generation and its effects on the traditional views of the decade. The author expresses his approval of this culture shift through symbolism that helps him to challenge the pervasive conformity of the 1950s. By leading his narrator out of the doldrums of A&P into the tumultuous and unfamiliar world of Queenie, Updike suggests the merits of disobedience and bohemianism and encourages the new generation of rebels.

Works Cited

Dougan, Clark and Samuel Lipsman. *A Nation Divided.* Boston: Boston Publishing Co., 1984. Print. The Vietnam Experience.

Ginsberg, Allen. "America." *Howl and Other Poems.* San Francisco, 1956. Al Filreis. University Web Space. "America." University of Pennsylvania, 22 Mar. 2009. Web. 12 Nov. 2014.

Holmes, John Clellon. "This Is The Beat Generation." Editorial. *The New York Times Magazine* 16 Nov. 1962: SM10. Print.

Updike, John. "A&P." *Making Literature Matter: An Anthology for Readers and Writers.* Ed. John Clifford and John Schilb. Boston: Bedford/St. Martin's, 2012. 614-619. Print.

Practice Makes Perfect

As I stated previously, revision was one of the most arduous tasks for me throughout this course. I tend to become attached to anything I write, which makes it challenging to revise or "scrap" any material. Of course, revision is an integral component of successful composition. If I want a decent essay, I must learn to accept when my writing is unsatisfactory. The following part of Paper 1 is an excellent illustration of how I overcame these challenges.

Key

Inadequate support

Ineffective grammar/syntax

Inadequate relation to thesis

Added/changed

Thesis

Through extensive symbolism and characterizations, Oates explores the age-old theme of independence and presents a vivid illustration of childish delusions versus the realities of adulthood.

Pre-write

Arnold Friend represents the maturity that Connie so fervently seeks. He serves as the embodiment of sensuality, offering Connie everything she desires: freedom (symbolized by the ostentatious golden jalopy), sex, and adventure. However, severed from the familiarity of family and home, Connie reverts back into a childlike state. As is the nature of the Beast, Connie's change in character is meaningless. She is thus uprooted from youth and forced into the alien lands of adulthood.

Process: I chose to include my pre-write with no color-coding to show the initial formation of my ideas. For this section of my essay, I wanted to show how Arnold Friend represents the allure that Connie mistakes for true independence. His mystery and audacity attract young Connie, and this attraction precipitates her downfall. I also wanted to explore the possibility of Friend being a biblical demon. To relate back to my thesis about the disparities between childish expectations and the realities of adulthood, I would include a description of Connie's attempt to return to childhood and her inability to escape Friend.

Draft 1

In her search for carte blanche, Connie attracts the strange Arnold Friend, who comes to represent everything Connie hopes to attain. As his name foreshadows, Friend treats his and Connie's young relationship with unwarranted intimacy. His first comment to her was an alarming "Gonna get you, baby" (1409), and when he later arrives unannounced, he asks her to "come for a ride" before even revealing his name (1411). This audacity coupled with an aura of mystery establishes Arnold Friend as the embodiment of Connie's desires. Arnold Friend represents the sensual and mysterious maturity that Connie so fervently seeks. He serves as the embodiment of carnality, offering Connie everything she desires: freedom (symbolized by the ostentatious golden jalopy), sex, and adventure. However, severed from the familiarity of family and home, Connie reverts back into a childlike state (the transformation complete when she "cried for her mother" (1418) over the telephone). As is the nature of the beast (Arnold Friend perhaps being the "Beast" himself), once Connie delved into depravity, she is uprooted from youth and forced into the alien lands of adulthood.

Process: This draft includes all of the ideas that I wanted to explore, but it was not as substantive as it should have been. I repeat several times that Friend is "the embodiment" of Connie's desires, but I do not specifically state the details that led me to this assertion. I needed to add more textual evidence to characterize Friend, specifically his other-worldliness. These details would act as a segue into my argument about Friend as a literal demon. I also briefly describe Connie's transition "back into a childlike state." However, I do not explicitly state the specifics of this transformation or how it relates to my thesis. Likewise, my concluding sentence indicates that Connie succumbed to Friend and must now face a dark unknown, but I do not mention how this relates to Oates's assertion concerning expectations versus the realities of adulthood.

Draft 2

In her search for carte blanche, Connie attracts the strange Arnold Friend, who comes to represent everything Connie hopes to attain. As his name foreshadows, Friend treats his and Connie's young relationship with unwarranted intimacy. His first comment to her is an alarming "Gonna get you, baby" (1409), and when he later arrives unannounced, he asks her to "come for a ride" before even revealing his name (1411). This audacity coupled with an aura of mystery establishes Arnold Friend as the embodiment of Connie's desires, namely freedom. Friend's ostentatious "convertible jalopy painted gold" (1409), complete with his name inscribed on the side, and a crude portrait of himself (1412), symbolizes Friend's enticing independence. In addition to his ability to traverse, Friend portrays himself as the perfect and normal rebellious youth. He dresses stylishly ("the way all of them dressed" (1412)) and appears to have all of the desirable attributes of the time. However, under the guise of the stereotype lies something sinister. Connie recognizes the familiarity of Friend's motions (his "sleepy, dreamy smile . . . the singsong way he talked . . . the way he tapped one fist against the other" (1414)), yet admits that these things did not come together" (1414). She remarks that "his whole face was a mask" (1416) and suggests several times that his hair is a wig. Following these accusations, Connie notes Friend's difficulty walking ("his feet did not go all the way down; his boots must have been stuffed with something" (1417)). Along with physical dissonance, Friend employs outdated colloquialisms, as though he was "no longer sure which one of them was in style" (1418). This observation in particular along with his difficulty walking suggest that Arnold Friend not only represents a beastly immorality, he represents the Beast himself. He preys on Connie and wears an attractive mask to engage her. He becomes the sensual and mysterious maturity that Connie so fervently seeks. He serves as the embodiment of carnality, offering Connie everything she desires: freedom, sex, and adventure. However, severed from the familiarity of family and home, Connie reverts back into a childlike state (the transformation complete when she "cried for her mother" (1418) over the telephone). As is the nature of the Beast, once Connie delved into depravity, she is uprooted from youth and forced into the alien lands of adulthood.

Process: In this draft, I focused on adding much more textual evidence. I knew I needed to provide more support for the assertions I made, such as Arnold Friend representing Connie's desires and the possibility of him being a literal demon. However, I still did not explicate the importance of Connie's reversion into infancy or how her forced departure from innocence contributed to my thesis.

Final Draft

In her search for autonomy, Connie attracts the strange Arnold Friend, who comes to represent everything Connie hopes to attain in adulthood. As his name foreshadows, Friend treats his and Connie's young relationship with unwarranted intimacy. His first comment to her is an alarming "Gonna get you, baby," and when he later arrives at her home unannounced, he offers to drive her away before even revealing his name (1409). This audacity coupled with an aura of mystery establishes Arnold Friend as the embodiment of Connie's desires, namely freedom. Friend's ostentatious "convertible jalopy painted gold," complete with his name inscribed on the side, and a crude portrait of himself, symbolizes Friend's enticing independence (1409). Unlike Connie, Arnold Friend is free to traverse without the boundaries of watchful family members or adult chauffeurs. Connie notes this nomadic spirit when she remarks that "he had driven up the driveway all right but had come from nowhere before that and belonged nowhere"(1415). It is this characteristic that enthralls Connie, leading her unknowingly to her ruination.

In addition to his freedom, of which Connie is certainly envious, Friend portrays himself as the perfect and normal rebellious youth. He dresses stylishly, notably "the way all of them dressed," and appears to have all of the desirable attributes of the time (1412). However, under the guise of the stereotype lies something sinister. Connie recognizes the familiarity of Friend's motions, such as his "sleepy, dreamy smile . . . the singsong way he talked . . . the way he tapped one fist against the other," yet she admits that "these things did not come together" (1414). She remarks that "his whole face was a mask" and suggests several times that his hair resembled a wig (1416). Following these accusations, Connie observes Friend's difficulty walking, noting "his feet did not go all the way down; his boots must have been stuffed with something" (1417). Along with physical dissonance, Friend layers outdated colloquialisms, as though he was "no longer sure which one of them was in style" (1418). He claims that he "[knows] everybody" and tells Connie that she has been marked with his sign—"an X in the air" (1413, 1414). This observation in particular suggests that Arnold Friend not only represents a beastly immorality, he represents the biblical Beast himself. Friend's difficulty walking implies cleft hooves, and his misuse of youthful phrases characterizes him as a calculating predator versed in aggressive mimicry. Like a mockingjay, he uses familiar calls to trick and ensnare his victims. He wears an attractive mask to exploit Connie's ignorance, and, once the mask is removed, escape is impossible.

Just as Connie fails to see of the negative aspects of adulthood, she is slow to realize Friend's devious intentions. Friend is the embodiment of carnality and presents Connie with everything she desires: freedom, sex, and adventure. It is not until Friend loses his charming facade that Connie understands the danger that confronts her. When he tells Connie "I'm your lover" and promises her that he will "hold you so tight you won't think you have to try to get away . . . because you know you can't," Connie finally recognizes Friend as an enemy (1416). In her desperation, she reaches out to figures of authority. Realizing that she has lost control, Connie threatens to call the police and insists that her father will soon come home (1416). These cries for help mark the beginning of Connie's regression into infancy. Severed from the familiarity of family and home, Connie abandons her glossy veneer and, at the climax of her transformation, "[cries] for her mother" over the telephone (1418). Despite Connie's anguish, Friend still forces upon her the life she once desired, thus uprooting Connie from youth and propelling her into the alien lands of adulthood.

Process: In this final draft, I realized that each detail I wanted to explore about Arnold Friend and Connie's relationship could easily become three separate paragraphs. The first describes Friend's allure and how he parallels Connie's desire for idealized independence. The second comments on Friend's other-worldliness and how these idiosyncrasies contribute to his status as a devil. The third paragraph chronicles how Connie abandons her search for independence and becomes a child in the face of danger. In addition to a change in structure, I included more specific details to further support each idea. I also replaced ineffective diction, changed all parenthetical statements to clauses separated by commas, and added transitional phrases to introduce each idea, which helped the paragraphs' "flow." Overall, my final draft became much more detailed. I wanted to ensure that my writing and support were clear enough to adequately express my thesis.

Reaching Out in the Dark

If nothing else, English 1102 has taught me the importance of peer review. As I stated in "Caving How-To,"I was skeptical when I first entered the course. It was difficult for me to accept criticism from someone sitting in the same desk as me. Likewise, I could not see why anyone would care about my comments either. Despite my reluctance, I still made a marked effort to supply substantive criticism for my review partners' Paper 1. Not surprisingly, it helped. In order to provide worthwhile comments, I had to understand the goals of my partner's essay as well as what our instructor expected of us. I tried to contribute constructive assessments that would bridge the gap between the student's and the instructor's goals.

I chose to present the following peer review because I believe it represents my most substantial critique. The author wanted to explore the unattainable nature of the American Dream in Arthur Miller's *Death of a Salesman*. To accomplish this, she provided character profiles for each member of the Loman family and explained how their current circumstances support the impracticality of traditional American "success." Though she had a solid argument and plan of action, her analysis could have been more substantial in some areas, and her diction was sometimes too colloquial. My comments aimed to improve both the content of her essay and its aesthetic quality.

Key

Ineffective/Awkward Diction

Unsupported Claim

Thesis

My comments

The American Dream or the American Nightmare?[1] I love this! So catchy!

The American Dream: it is an idea that has been rooted in this great nation since the beginning of its creation[2] This may be a bit redundant. You could probably just say "its beginning" or "its creation." European men and women ventured here in flee of religious persecution and governmental oppression while Asian and Hispanic people came in pursuit of economic opportunity. The common notion is that as soon as one gets here life becomes simple—that he or she will "get rich quick." However, many quickly learn that the American Dream is not all it is cracked up to be . Arthur Miller's *Death of a Salesman* tells the story of a dysfunctional family whose father, Willy Loman, holds an unreasonable belief that his son Biff will one day "end up big" (Miller 98). However, Biff and Happy, the other, younger son, accomplish nothing, failing to live up to Willy's enormous expectations. Through Miller's characterization of the Loman family, he critiques the reality of the American Dream by suggesting that no matter how hard one works there is a chance that one can still fail. Ultimately, true success is not determined by one's job, money, or standard or living, but rather it is determined by how content one is with the life he or she is living.

There are many words that can be used to describe Willy Loman: troubled, hard-working, stubborn, and unstable[3] Maybe you could add a bit of analysis at the end of this statement. You describe him, then add a phrase to explain what this description means. "Willy is self-deluded, believing wholeheartedly in the American Dream of success and wealth" (Sickels 84)[4] Maybe add some of your own words around this quote so it does not stand alone. His entire world revolves around Biff because he relies on the belief that his son is too great of a man to be considered a failure. To him, "the man who makes an appearance in the business world" holds the key to success; therefore, as long as Biff looks and acts the part he will be "the man who gets ahead" (Miller 33). All the while throughout[5] This sounds a bit redundant. You could probably just say "Thoughout" or "During his son's..." his son's trials in various jobs, Willy continues to believe that Biff is too good—too important for an average, low-income lifestyle. Willy's "feeling of entitlement, that if [he] plays by the rules [he] will in time reap his... just rewards, [has] led [him]... astray" from the realities of life (Samuel 7)[6] This quote sounds a bit awkward. Maybe you could quote the important parts, then paraphrase the rest. This illusion of the American Dream tricks Willy into thinking that a life in sales, like his own, will provide his sons with substantial and happy lives, but in actuality he is only fooling himself. The irony lies in the fact that Willy, who works like a dog[7] Maybe include specific details to support this? to provide for his family and must also go to excruciating ends for them, ultimately causes Biff to neglect him by acting as an overbearing father. Willy's suicide goes to show that no matter how hard one works throughout the course of his or her life, he or she is not guaranteed happiness. In the end, Willy dies believing in the American Dream, although he nor his sons never have nor will live it.

In response to everything Willy Loman wants him to be, Biff is the opposite. He is seen by Wily "as an underachiever," but what sets him apart is his "refus[al] to be self-deceived by his father's unrealistic dreams (Sickels 85). Unlike the other characters in the story, Biff undergoes a unique transformation that sets him a part.[8] How specifically is he different? Through Miller's use of flashbacks, we see Biff's former self several times throughout the story through Willy's flashbacks. In these scenes, the audience sees Biff as an eager young man who would do anything to please his father, even if it means "break[ing] through for a touchdown" for him (Miller 32). However, as the story progresses the reader learns of the cheating scandal and Biff's involvement in it, and things are never the same. Biff flunks out of high school because he is too disgusted by father. He has lost so much respect for Willy that he refuses to let him do the simplest of things for him, even calling the school to get him passed. From here on out, Biff rejects his father and calls him a "phony dream[er]" (Miller 133). Biff, who is characterized as a strong, well-built young man, has many things going for him and supposed to be destined for success, but ironically ends up as a bum. This illustrates the fact that the American Dream is not destined for everyone.

Happy is a combination of his father and Biff's characteristics.[9] How does this characterization relate to your argument? Like Biff, he too is somewhat of a failure, for he is an attention-seeking compulsive liar who does not have much of a job either. Miller uses repetition to show how Happy so grovels for Willy's attention. For example, several times throughout the story Happy repeats the phrases "I'm losing weight, you notice, Pop?" and "I'm getting married, Pop" (Miller 29, 133). Because he takes after his father so much, Happy "deludes [himself]" into believing that Biff and he have a real shot in the business world (Sickels 85). Like Willy, Happy completely believes in the American Dream and refuses to accept the fact that he and Biff are utter failures.

Finally, the last member of the family is Willy's wife, Linda[10] Maybe here you could go ahead and introduce how her characterization supports your thesis?. In essence, she is Willy's only true support system because she do whatever he tells her. She, too, "believes in the American Dream, but she is more grounded than her husband " and glues the family together by serving as "the emotional core" (Sickels 85).

It goes without saying Willy Loman wanted the best for his sons. Was it so wrong for him to force his hopes and dreams upon them? Is that not what all fathers and mothers do to their children anyway? Tragically, his goals for his sons were far-fetched—hidden in a "jungle... full of diamonds,"[11] Try adding some explanation here. What exactly is this jungle? Willy continued to believe in the American Dream even in his death, refusing to accept the fact that his sons were simply average just like he[12] This sounds a bit odd. I'm not sure, but I think "he" should be "him." I would check!. By having Biff reach the conclusion that he is meant for the farmland lifestyle, Miller suggests that one[13] Since you follow this pronoun with others like "his" and "he," maybe consider changing "one" to "a person" or "a man." should follow his passions rather than trying to be something he is not. Willy's downfall lies in the fact that he cannot accept this idea.

Strengths: Good topic! Lots of potential support. Also, I like the way you divided the paper into individual characterizations.

Weaknesses: Your characterizations and analysis seem to dwindle with each body paragraph. Try adding more support especially for Happy and Linda.

Unexpected Rises and Drops

During high school, I was lucky to have wonderful English and literature teachers. Though creative writing was not a large part of the standards for any course, many teachers sought to improve our writing skills and thought processes through entertaining and low-stakes techniques. One year, our instructor introduced us to a creative writing technique she called "blind writing." She told us to sit at a computer, open a Word document, and turn off the monitor. As the name suggests, blind writing is done blindly. Along with the monitor, she also told us to turn off our "internal editors." Write exactly what you think. There are no mistakes, no proper formats, nothing. There are only thoughts.

For my Wild Card, I chose to revisit this technique. Over the course of one week, I dedicated ten to fifteen minutes each night to blind writing. What follows are some of the resulting unedited monologues. While writing, I did not give much thought to grammar or syntax, and when there was a lull in my thoughts, I immediately started a new line. I believe this technique allowed me to truly showcase both personality and thought process.

November 14, 2014

A ball ticks ticks ticks

Down down down

The ceaseless stairs staring straight

Into infinity

It slows and softens

Thunk thunk

It sinks and stretches

Pretty and primordial

Until

Slam Squashed Sandwiched

There goes the ball

There goes the block

Sailing sailing sailing

Innards jumble

And shift and stand, screaming

For their mother

November 17, 2014

I eat salads because they taste like dirt

And nine-year-old faces on the concrete, the lower-lip sting, the teeth indent felt for days,

The pink knees that hiss under hydrogen peroxide and bites that whither under alcohol

I eat salads because they remind me that I am still a child, that the pink knees never really healed and the pavement still beckons for a tender mouth to make tough

November 19, 2014

I want to stand on top of a mountain and scream my name to the sun until its rays stop for a moment and think "who is this that disrupts Our majesty?" *I will announce to the world that I am here in all my ugly beauty,* says my wishful brain today, but tomorrow I am content balancing on a white picket fence.

I should have more to say, I should have an implacable fire inside of me, both quelled and ignited by blick pens run dry.

But here I sit wondering what my next words will be, surprised by my proverbial pen strokes, my brain quiet like the night.

Appendix

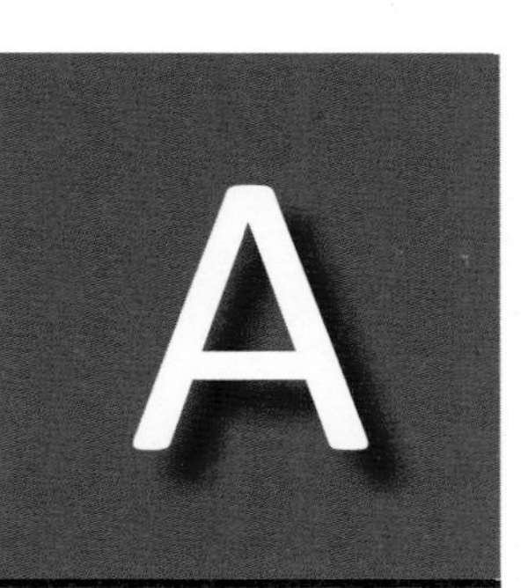

Learning (Your First Job)

by Robert Leamnson, PhD

Introduction (Don't skip this part)

These pages contain some fairly blunt suggestions about what to do in college. Some of them may seem strange to you, some might seem old fashioned, and most will come across as labor intensive. But they have worked very well for many students over the past 20 years, since the first edition came out. This edition is more up to date, but the basic message has not changed much.

A fundamental idea that you will encounter over and again, is that learning is not something that just happens to you, it is something that *you do to yourself*. You cannot be "given" learning, nor can you be forced to do it. The most brilliant and inspired teacher cannot "cause" you to learn. Only you can do that. What follows are some fairly explicit "learning activities" or behaviors, but they are all *your* activities, and now and then those of your fellow students. But there is also a basic assumption underlying these ideas, and that's that you do want to learn something while getting a diploma. Without that desire, nothing will work.

Some words we need to understand

It happens, too often, that someone reads a passage or paragraph, as you are, and gets an idea very different from what the writer intended. This is almost always because the reader has somewhat different meanings for the words than did the writer. So that we don't have that problem here I'll make clear the meanings I intend by the words I use. We'll start with:

Learning

While few people think of it this way, learning is a biological process. It is indeed biological because thinking occurs when certain webs (networks) of neurons (cells) in your brain begin sending signals to other webs of neurons. You, of course, are not conscious of this process, but only of the thought that results. But there is no doubt that thinking is the result of webs of cells in your brain sending signals to other webs.

How can knowing what causes thought help in the learning process? Start by considering that human learning has two components:

1) Understanding

2) Remembering

Either of these by itself is not sufficient. Knowing a bit about how the brain works when you're thinking will help you to see why *both* understanding and remembering are necessary for learning.

Anytime you encounter a new idea (and that, after all, is why you are in college) you need to "make sense" of it, or, to understand it. And if you are actually *trying* to make sense of it, your brain is firing a lot of webs of neurons until one or more of them "sees" the logic or causality in a situation. Understanding sometimes comes in a flash and we feel, "Oh, I get it!" Other times it takes repeated exposure or the use of analogies until we finally "get it." But if we *never* get it, then we still don't understand—we haven't tried enough circuits in the brain.

So, right from the beginning, making sense of what you read or hear involves focused attention and concentration, in other words, "brain work." I'm confident that almost all college students "could" understand what is required of them by focusing attention on what is being read or heard, and stick with it until the thoughts in their heads pretty much matched those of the speaker or writer.

Unhappily, this is not the way all students in college behave. The most frequent complaint I hear from college instructors is that too many of their students are simply "passive observers." So the big rule about understanding is that it *cannot* be achieved passively. It demands an active and focused mind.

Some very bright students find little difficulty in understanding what they hear or read. But some of these smart people get very poor grades and sometimes drop out. The reason is, they neglect the second part of learning, which is *remembering*.

For most people, I suspect, remembering is more difficult than understanding. I would suggest that this is because few people know much about memory, or that it is likewise a biological process involving the firing of webs of neurons in the brain. Most people think of memories as ideas, pictures, or events that are lodged somewhere in their heads, and these places simply need to be "found." The fact, however, is that memories are not things always present somewhere in our heads. Memories must be *reconstructed* each time they are remembered. This reconstruction, in biological terms, means firing up almost the same webs of neurons that were used to perceive the original event. This would seem to be easy, but it is not in most cases. Here's the reason.

Use it or lose it

These webs I've been speaking of are networks of connected neurons. The details do not need to be understood, but the fact is, the *connections* between brain cells are not necessarily permanent. *Much of our brain is not hard wired*. One can think of neurons as having a big, important rule, "if the connection I made gets used a lot, it must be doing something important or useful, so I will strengthen the connection so it doesn't fall apart." And that's exactly what it does (even though, in fact, it itself doesn't *know* what it's doing.) Now the bad news. If a neuron makes a connection that does not get used (no matter how useful it *might have been*) it breaks the connection and it's probably gone forever. In short, neural circuits that get used become stable, those that do not get used fall apart.

So it is that we can understand something quite clearly, and some time later not be able to remember what it was we understood. The biological explanation is that the "web of understanding" was not used enough to become stable, so it fell apart.

If you've followed all of this you probably see the bad news coming. If learning means *both* understanding and remembering, we have to *practice* what we understand. Without rehearsal, that fantastic circuitry that enabled our understanding will gradually disintegrate and we can no longer reconstruct what we once understood.

If learning means both understanding and remembering, we have to practice what we understand.

Some readers are no doubt wanting to get on to the "tricks" for getting high grades. But for a lot of college courses, getting a high grade involves *only* one trick—learn the material. Learning, as described here, is the trick that always works.

Learning is the goal—keep that always in mind through the rest of these pages. Grades will take care of themselves.

The Classroom

The classroom might be very traditional—a collection of students in chairs and an instructor at the front—or people seated at computer terminals, or alone at home with the computer. So long as these are in some way "interactive" with an instructor, the following suggestions will be valid and useful.

The reason something must be said about so commonplace a thing as the classroom is that too many students see it incorrectly and so they waste a highly valuable occasion for learning. The most common misconception is that the class period is that occasion when the instructor tells you what you need to know to pass the tests. Seen this way, it can only be a dreary thing, and from this perception flow a number of bad habits and behaviors that make learning more laborious and less interesting that it can be and should be.

"Taking" notes

I would like to see the expression "taking notes" removed from the vocabulary and replaced with one often used in Great Britain, that is "making notes." "Taking" implies a passive reception of something someone else has made. It too often consists of copying what's on a chalkboard or being projected on a screen.

Copying from a projected image is usually quite difficult and trying to copy what someone is saying is nearly impossible. Attempts to take notes in this way produces something that is usually quite incomplete, often garbled and has the awful effect of turning off the *listening* part of the brain. We are not capable of focusing attention on two different activities at the same time. So we miss what an instructor is saying while we concentrate on writing what he has already said, or copying from the board or screen. Some instructors compensate by making notes *for* the students and passing them out. This practice can help the better students—those who already know how to learn—but for many others it only makes matters worse. For a passive person, having a set of teacher-prepared notes means that they now have *nothing* to do during the class period. So they just sit, or daydream, or doze off, and often quit coming to class altogether. Why not, if it's all in the notes? Two more definitions will help to see that this is a recipe for failure.

Information and Knowledge

Even college professors and authors of books often confuse these words or use them interchangeably. In fact they mean very different things. Let's start with information. The world is awash in information. All the books in the library have information, as do journals, magazines, and the uncountable number of websites and postings on the internet. All of this information is transferable from one medium to another, sometimes with lightening speed. *None of it, however, is knowledge!* The reason being that knowledge can only exist in someone's head. Furthermore, the expression "transfer of knowledge" is ridiculous because it describes the impossible.

This might be a novel or surprising idea so let's examine it further. Suppose your chemistry teacher has a correct and fairly thorough knowledge of oxidation/reduction reactions. Can this knowledge be transferred to you? How wonderful if it could be. Something like a "transfusion" or "mind meld" and you know instantly what he/she knows! None of that is possible. All your teacher can give you is *information*, and perhaps the inspiration for you to do your part. This information is always in the form of symbols. These symbols might be words,—spoken or written—numbers, signs, diagrams, pictures, and so on. You cannot learn anything unless you have previous knowledge of the meaning of the symbols. As a clear example, you cannot learn from someone speaking Farsi if you know only English, no matter how accurate and useful the information embedded in that language. This idea—new knowledge depends greatly on prior knowledge—will come up again later.

But if, happily, you can indeed "make sense" of new information on chemical reactions (or anything else) you can then construct your own knowledge by using the new information and incorporating it into your prior knowledge base. But, as noted above, this will involve using some not-used-before neural connections, so if you want to *remember* what you now *understand*, you must practice, that is review a number of times, or use the new knowledge repeatedly to solve problems or answer questions. Remember the rule about new knowledge—use it or lose it.

Remember the new rule about knowledge - use it or lose it.

So, what do I have to do?

All of this talk about brains, information, and knowledge is not just abstract theory. It *is* the way we learn. The way to learn, then, is to align your own activities with those behaviors we already know will work.

Time

Time is nothing at all like the way we talk about it. How often do you hear someone say that they "didn't have time?" It's a perfectly meaningless expression. When you wake up on a Sunday morning, you have exactly 168 hours of time until the following

Sunday morning. And everybody on the planet gets 168 hours. *No one ever has any more or any less time than anyone else!* Time cannot be "found," nor "stretched," nor "compressed," nor "lost." It cannot be "saved" or "bought," or in any other way "managed" for any realistic meaning of the word "manage." So why do we use all these meaningless expressions? It's because they let us avoid the embarrassing process of examining our priorities, a ranked list of those things we hold to be important. Sleeping is a high priority for everyone—it's a biological necessity, like food—so we all spend a fair amount of our allotted time blissfully unconscious. Now, what about the rest of our 168 hours? For someone who has to work part time to meet expenses, work is a high priority activity and they show up on schedule and on time because losing the job would mean losing the income and the consequences would be serious. So, after sleeping, eating, working, and, one hopes, going to classes, the rest of our 168 hours are spent doing whatever we find personally important. For some, doing assignments, reading books, writing reports and the like are important, so they always get done. For some others, TV, "hanging out," the internet, and partying are of primary importance, and sometimes they fill up so many of the 168 hours available that there is nothing left at the end of the week. Remember, no one gets more than 168 hours, so anyone who thinks they can "do it all" is *always* going to "run out of time."

It's your priorities and not the clock that will determine the outcome of your college experience. If it's really important, it will always get done, and always at the expense of the less important.

Studying

You and your teachers will use the word "study" frequently, and always assuming that it means the same thing to everyone. But it doesn't. For way too many college students, particularly in the first year, study never happens until just before a test. Teachers are amazed at the idea, but many students simply see no reason to study if there is no test on the horizon. So here in a nutshell is a most serious misunderstanding between college teachers and beginning students. For teachers, the purpose of study is to understand and remember the course content; for students the purpose of study is to pass the tests.

Now in an ideal world these would amount to the same thing. But in the real world, unfortunately, you can pass some tests without learning much at all. This is not the place for me to beat up on my colleagues, but some do produce truly simple-minded exams that do not require much by way of preparation. So here's an absolutely *heroic* idea if you find yourself bored with a class; try learning more than the teacher demands. Wake up your childhood curiosity and ask why other people find this discipline so interesting that they spend their lives at it. I can about guarantee that there are bright, articulate, and interesting writers in every college discipline. Find a good book and read. That way you'll learn something even if the teacher doesn't demand it.

If you find yourself bored with a class, try learning more than the teacher demands.

But such "gut" courses might be rare in your college. The ones that cause trouble and hurt the grade point average are those where the teacher expects serious learning, but leaves most of it up to you. How do you cope with that?

Tough Courses

What makes a course tough? Well, sometimes it only means large amounts of material, many pages to read, lots of writing assignments, and the like. But the really tough course is one where the subject itself is complex, or presents difficult problems for the learner to deal with, and often goes faster than students would find comfortable. Suppose we add to that a super-smart teacher, but one who simply assumes you know how to learn, and sprays information like a fire hose.

For a typical first year student this is the famous "worst case scenario." The whole purpose of my writing is to help you cope with worst case scenarios.

During the Lecture

In these tough courses the first idea you must abandon is that you can sit, "take" notes, and worry about it later. Here's another key idea to bring with you to every lecture period. *Worry about it* ***now***.

You can look upon your teacher as an adversary, something that stands between you and a diploma, but that's a defeatist and erroneous idea. It's better to think of the instructor as your private tutor. Most teachers welcome a considered question on the content. They nearly all resent questions like, "is this going to be on the test?" You don't do yourself any favors by giving your teachers the impression that you're a lazy goof off trying to slide by with minimal effort. Teachers can often pack a wealth of important information in what just sounds like an interesting story. They do not seem to be "giving notes." It's a serious mistake to get comfortable and daydream. When notes are not "given," then you have to make them, and that's anything but relaxing. It takes careful listening, concentration, and a focused mind to pick out the important nuggets from what appears to be a non-stop verbal ramble. A casual remark like, "there are several reasons we believe these things happen," is a clear clue that something worth knowing is coming. As noted, some teachers may pass out notes that they have made, and these might contain an outline of what's important. A fair number of college faculty have learned that this only encourages passivity and cutting classes. (It's quite easy to get the notes from someone else, and if it's only the notes that are important, why spend time sitting in a classroom?) Some teachers have discovered that students can only be prodded to serious mental activity if they *don't* provide prepared notes. This might seem mean spirited to you, but they're just trying to activate your brain.

Here's another strange but important truth; all of your interests had to be learned.

Under conditions described above, you, to make notes from which you can learn, have to be attuned to what's being said. Not every sentence that drops from an instructor's mouth is going to contain some pearl of wisdom. Much of it is "filler"—rephrasing, giving examples, preparatory remarks for the next point and so on. You have to learn quickly where the gems are. Sentences you hear stay in the short term, immediate recall part of your brain for only a couple seconds. During that brief time you have to make the decision as to whether you've heard something important or just filler. If it was important you have to get the gist into your notes, even if that means not being quite so attentive so far as listening goes. Once it's down, refocus and wait for the next useful idea.

In short, teachers who do not "make it easy" by doing all the work, are, in fact, doing you a favor. What is often called "deep learning," the kind that demands both understanding and remembering of relationships, causes, effects and implications for new or different situations simply *cannot be made easy.* Such learning depends on students actually *restructuring* their brains and that demands effort.

Such learning can, however, be most satisfying and enjoyable, even as it demands effort. I always think of serious learning of any academic subject as being something like practice for a sport or with a musical instrument. No one is born with a genetic endowment for playing either the trombone or ice hockey. These are both *developed* skills and both take long periods of concentration and effort. Both are simply difficult, but how satisfying they are as small elements are learned and burned into our brain circuits! How enjoyable to become proficient! It's exactly the same with academic matters. Give it a try.

About Interests

An obvious response to the thoughts just expressed might be, "but I like hockey, I have no interest in history," or chemistry—whatever. That may well be true, but what is *not true* is the assumption that these interests are natural—something you came into the world with. Here's another strange but important truth; *all of your interests had to be learned!* This is a small example of a paradox. You need to *know something* about a musical instrument, or a sport, or indeed, an academic subject, before you can judge whether or not it's interesting. But if you hold the belief that you cannot learn anything *until* or *unless* it's interesting, then you can never get started on anything new.

I was always impressed with my senior biology majors who came to my office and got around to talking about their courses in psychology, or philosophy, or art history. These students gave every discipline a chance to prove itself. Instead of depending on a teacher to "make it interesting," they studied it on their own to discover why other folk found it interesting enough to write books about it, and teach it in college. You would do yourself a great favor by developing this "curiosity habit" as early on as you can.

Between Classes

When a teacher happens not to assign some specific work to be done for the next period, a disturbing number of beginning students simply assume that means that nothing at all needs to be done. And it so happens that a lot of college instructors *do not assign* each time some reading, or writing, or problem solving to be done. And if you had an orientation session, someone probably told you that "they" expected you to spend three hours on each of your subjects, *for each hour in class!* That usually comes to an amazing 45 hours a week. Most students find that unreasonable and unnecessary, and I tend to agree. But the proper response to an excessive demand is not to do *nothing*. A huge number of new college students, when told to *study* but given nothing specific to do, simply do nothing. So here are some realistic suggestions for study outside class time.

Fill in the Notes

As noted above, it's essential during a lecture to produce some record, no matter how sketchy, of what was presented during that period. A most useful and highly recommended way so spend half an hour or so of study time is to make sense of these notes, and most importantly, turn lists and key words into real sentences that rephrase what went on. When memory fails, that's the time to use resources. Sometimes your best resource is the textbook. Even if no pages were assigned directly, there is a very high probability that the text contains, somewhere, a good, or better, description of what the teacher had presented. You may have to search for it, but tables of contents, chapter headings and the index will lead you to what you need.

Now, read with the intent of re-discovering what was presented in class. Read with understanding as the goal (this will *feel* different than reading because it was assigned.) People who know the education process thoroughly say that *most* learning in college goes on outside the classroom. So it is that you will know *more* about the day's material after this "filling in" process than when you first heard it.

But there is a further critical element here. You must *write* in your notes, in real sentences, what you have learned by the reading. Writing has an enormous power to *fix* things in the mind. *Always* write what you have learned. (Once in a while a short paragraph that summarizes or paraphrases an important aspect becomes exactly what you need on an exam. You will almost certainly remember it because you've already written it before.) There are two other good resources for filling in the notes should the textbook be insufficient. These are your classmates and the teacher (or tutor if one is available.)

Huge studies have been done to find out just what "works" for college students. What, in other words, did the truly successful students actually *do* that the unsuccessful ones did not? The first of the two most outstanding findings was that successful students had gotten "connected" to those of their teachers who were open to talking with students (and there are a lot of these.) The intent was not merely social. The point was to become more familiar with course content by simply discussing it with an expert.

Remember, the successful students said that this was the *most important* thing they did to be successful. So you don't have to wonder about it; the experiment's already been done.

The second most important activity for success was to form small study groups, or pairs, with the express purpose of talking about the course content, their notes, and assigned work. Working together on assignments and problems is not cheating. Copying without learning is cheating. Discussing the details of an assignment or problem is just cooperative learning—one of the most useful habits you can develop in college. (I'm perfectly aware, by the way, that getting some guys together to discuss psychology sounds like a pretty "nerdy" thing to do. Well, so what? Really smart college students have no problem stealing a page from the "Nerd's Handbook" if it means learning more and doing better.)

Assignments

Here again, attitude will influence how you react to assigned work. To view it as paying dues, or taxes, or as mere busywork that teachers insist on out of habit, is to squander an excellent learning opportunity. Inexperienced students see assignments as something to be *done*; experienced students see them as something to be *used*. Look on every assignment as a clue from the teacher—what he or she considers important enough to spend time learning. Assignments, in most cases, are solid, meaty chunks of what's important. Don't just *do* assignments with minimal effort and thought, *use* them to learn something new.

Always write what you have learned.

Thoughts on verbalization

Here's another experiment that's already been done and you won't have to repeat. Things do not go into memory as a result of thinking about them vaguely—in the abstract. It has been well documented that *thought*, to be useful, must be *verbal*. Now all that means is that, to be remembered, and so useful, your thought on a topic needs to be either spoken, aloud, to another person, or written on paper. (Recall the earlier idea that information can only *move* by means of symbols, words spoken, signed, or written.) In either case, good English sentences are needed—not just word clusters. You need *verbs*. Who did what to whom? How does this thing cause that thing to happen? These facts support the suggested need to talk to teachers and classmates and use writing assignments to say what's true or useful. And here's a bonus! If you have filled in your notes and discussed a topic with a classmate, even if it only took 30 minutes, you will be *prepared* for the next class. That means you will have something to say should there be a "pop quiz," or if the teacher starts asking questions. Or, just as well, you can start the class by asking a well-prepared question on the last period's material. Trust me—the teacher will notice, and remember, favorably.

Learn as you go means you're always prepared.

Access and high technology

There have been some noisy claims that today's students will turn out to be the best educated so far, *because* they have access (by way of the internet) to unimaginably more information than any previous generation. I have reservations about this claim for several reasons. For one thing, the internet has been with us for quite some time, and those of us who teach college are still looking for the promised improvement. Results should have showed up by now.

The principal reason, however, goes back to the fundamental difference between *information* and *knowledge*. Knowledge is what has the potential for improving the individual and society. But websites are completely devoid of knowledge; all they have is information (and not all of that is reliable!) No matter how many websites you have access to, none of them can do anything for you unless you can make sense of (and evaluate) what you find there.

And here is another little paradox I discovered by observing the differences between accomplished college seniors and most first year students. Instead of getting knowledge from the internet, *you need to have a lot of knowledge beforehand* to make sense of the ocean of information you find there.

It's tempting to believe that access to more information is going to make college easy. But it's just a temptation. You fall for it at your peril. The internet is a tool, and a very useful one, but as with all tools, you have to be knowledgeable to use it profitably.

Exams

I have intentionally put last what most new college students consider to be the single most important aspect of college—tests and exams. My reason for this approach is simple. If you attend class regularly, listen with attention, make the best notes you can, fill them in later (preferably with a study partner or two), verbalize your thoughts, and use assignments as learning tools, then you would be ready for a test at any time. Learn as you go means you're always prepared.

That is, of course, a bit overstated. In the real world, a "big test" in the offing makes even the best student nervous, and everyone bears down to some degree to get prepared. For someone who has done it all wrong, whose notes are just words copied without context or explanation, who does nothing between classes, and who never discusses coursework with anyone, and who does assignments thoughtlessly—just to have something to pass in—an upcoming exam is justifiably terrifying. It's these students who do everything wrong who ask embarrassing questions like, "What's this test going to cover?" or, "What chapters should we study?" They're clueless and they know it.

But let's assume you've done all the right things. You still want to do the best you can, and that means review, because stuff tends to slip out of memory, particularly when you have three or four other classes to attend to. But I mean "review" literally. It means learn again, not learn for the first time. No one can "learn" the content of 15 or 20 lectures in two days. Unless it's all completely trivial, that just can't be done. Learning a second time (real review), on the other hand, is a snap compared to learning from scratch. So, review for an exam *should not be stressful*. If you're in a state of panic because of an exam it's because you've been doing the wrong things all along.

But you're smart. You've done the right things. How do you do the review?

Don't go it alone

If you've done the right things you already have a study partner or two. Schedule firm times and places to spend an hour or so reviewing. Estimate how many days it will take to review all the material and get an early start. Don't worry about reviewing too far in advance of the exam! If you talk about the content and *write* summary paragraphs or descriptions, make labeled diagrams, or solve problems on paper, you won't forget—it's guaranteed. Remember, stealing a "nerd trick" will make you a better student.

Get Satan behind thee

The absolute worst thing you can do is to fall for the crazy notion that the way to prepare for an exam is to compress it all in the last 12 to 18 hours before the test, and keep it up right to the very last minute. I could always predict with great accuracy who was going to do poorly on an exam. They were red-eyed, gulping coffee to stay awake, and frantically flipping pages even as the test papers were being distributed. They had done it all wrong.

"Pulling an all-nighter," as the cute expression has it, is based on the completely erroneous belief that the only thing that college work requires is short term memory. Were that true, "last minute" study would make at least some sense. But the truth is, most college work demands thinking about, and using, a storehouse of information firmly lodged in long term memory. "All-nighter" students can usually recall a lot of terms and certain "facts," but can't do anything with them.

Trying to study 12 hours without sleep has the same effect on your brain as trying to play basketball for 12 straight hours would have on the rest of your body.

Remember, your thinking and remembering are functions of your brain, and that's a biological organ, and significantly, it's one with limited endurance. In short, it becomes less efficient the longer you put demands on it without rest. Trying to study 12 hours without sleep has the same effect on your brain as trying to play basketball for 12 straight hours would have on the rest of your body.

So, a final rule: "Always get a night of restful sleep the night before an exam." Some students are afraid of this rule. They are afraid that sleep will somehow wipe out all they've been studying. But it doesn't! It's another of those things that have been researched and the results are consistent. There is, in fact, a small but significant increase in the ability to recall or reconstruct when learning is followed by sleep. So if you want your brain in tip-top condition for an exam (and who wouldn't?) do your reviewing in one or two hour periods spread out over several days, and get a real night's sleep before the exam.

During the exam

I've heard students, going into an exam, say, "I've done my part; it's out of my hands now." That idea betrays the erroneous notion that all the hard work is done in advance, and during the exam you just pour out what you've learned. Well, sometimes. But exams in the tough courses often shock beginning students because they can't find much that looks familiar. There's a reason, and a solution.

Demanding teachers prepare exams that require performance, where performance is much more than recall. A lot of college instructors produce what might be called "application questions" for their exams. All that means is that you can't just write what you know, you have to use what you know to answer a question or solve a problem that you haven't seen before. Only a malicious teacher would question students on material that had never been discussed, assigned, or included in required reading. It seldom happens. So when seeing something that looks unfamiliar, convince yourself that it's only a question that is asking you to apply something you already know. So it is that concentration and focused thinking are often just as necessary during an exam as before it. If you have learned well, and reviewed properly, you can be confident that you have the necessary knowledge. It just takes some hard thinking to see how it applies to a particular question.

A Summary

No one learns unless they want to. I have assumed here that you do. But learning is a biological process that relies on the brain, a physiological organ that demands the same maintenance the rest of you does. Don't abuse it. The best ways to learn have already been discovered, there's no need for you to rediscover them by making a lot of old mistakes all over again. So it is that what you read here might be disappointing. Instead of new tricks or clever ways to beat the system, it says learning is the only way, and that learning is difficult and requires effort. But we do know how to do it, and when it's done right, it is marvelously satisfying.

I wish all readers of these pages the best of luck in their college days. But as I do so, I'm reminded of the words of the biologist Pasteur who said, "Chance favors the prepared mind."

Robert Leamnson

Dartmouth MA Dec. 2002

How is college different from high school?

FOLLOWING THE RULES IN HIGH SCHOOL	CHOOSING RESPONSIBLY IN COLLEGE
High school is mandatory and usually free.	College is voluntary and expensive.
Your time is structured by others.	You manage your own time.
You need permission to participate in extracurricular activities.	You must decide whether to participate in co-curricular activities.
You can count on parents and teachers to remind you of your responsibilities and guide you in setting priorities.	You must balance your responsibilities and set priorities. You will face moral and ethical decisions you have never faced before.
Each day you proceed from one class directly to another, spending 6 hours each day--30 hours a week--in class.	You often have hours between classes; class times vary throughout the day and evening and you spend only 12 to 16 hours each week in class.
Most of your classes are arranged for you.	You arrange your own schedule in consultation with your adviser. Schedules tend to look lighter than they really are.
You are not responsible for knowing what it takes to graduate.	Graduation requirements are complex, and differ from year to year. You are expected to know those that apply to you.
Guiding principle: You will usually be told what to do and corrected if your behavior is out of line.	**Guiding principle:** You are expected to take responsibility for what you do and don't do, as well as for the consequences of your decisions.

How is college different from high school?

Going to High School Classes	Succeeding in College Classes
The school year is 36 weeks long; some classes extend over both semesters and some don't.	The academic year is divided into two separate 15-week semesters, plus a week after each semester for exams.
Classes generally have no more than 35 students.	Classes may number 100 students or more.
You may study outside class as little as 0 to 2 hours a week, and this may be mostly last-minute test preparation.	You need to study at least 2 to 3 hours outside of class for each hour in class.
You seldom need to read anything more than once, and sometimes listening in class is enough.	You need to review class notes and text material regularly.
You are expected to read short assignments that are then discussed, and often re-taught, in class.	You are assigned substantial amounts of reading and writing which may not be directly addressed in class.
Guiding principle: You will usually be told in class what you need to learn from assigned reading.	**Guiding principle:** College is a learning environment in which you take responsibility for thinking through and applying what you have learned.

HOW IS COLLEGE DIFFERENT FROM HIGH SCHOOL?

HIGH SCHOOL TEACHERS	COLLEGE PROFESSORS
Teachers check your completed homework.	Professors may not always check completed homework, but they will assume you can perform the same tasks on tests
Teachers remind you of your incomplete work.	Professors may not remind you of incomplete work.
Teachers approach you if they believe you need assistance.	Professors are usually open and helpful, but most expect you to initiate contact if you need assistance.
Teachers are often available for conversation before, during, or after class.	Professors expect and want you to attend their scheduled office hours.
Teachers have been trained in teaching methods to assist in imparting knowledge to students	Professors have been trained as experts in their particular areas of research.
Teachers provide you with information you missed when you were absent.	Professors expect you to get from classmates any notes from classes you missed.
Teachers present material to help you understand the material in the textbook.	Professors may not follow the textbook. Instead, to amplify the text, they may give illustrations, provide background information, or discuss research about the topic you are studying. Or they may expect you to relate the classes to the textbook readings.

How is college different from high school?

HIGH SCHOOL TEACHERS	COLLEGE PROFESSORS
Teachers often write information on the board to be copied in your notes.	Professors may lecture nonstop, expecting you to identify the important points in your notes. When professors write on the board, it may be to amplify the lecture, not to summarize it. Good notes are a must.
Teachers impart knowledge and facts, sometimes drawing direct connections and leading you through the thinking process.	Professors expect you to think about and synthesize seemingly unrelated topics.
Teachers often take time to remind you of assignments and due dates.	Professors expect you to read, save, and consult the course syllabus (outline); the syllabus spells out exactly what is expected of you, when it is due, and how you will be graded.
Teachers carefully monitor class attendance.	Professors may not formally take roll, but they are still likely to know whether or not you attended.
Guiding principle: High school is a teaching environment in which you acquire facts and skills.	**Guiding principle:** College is a learning environment in which you take responsibility for thinking through and applying what you have learned.

How is college different from high school?

TESTS IN HIGH SCHOOL	TESTS IN COLLEGE
Testing is frequent and covers small amounts of material.	Testing is usually infrequent and may be cumulative, covering large amounts of material. You, not the professor, need to organize the material to prepare for the test. A particular course may have only 2 or 3 tests in a semester.
Makeup tests are often available.	Makeup tests are seldom an option; if they are, you need to request them.
Teachers frequently rearrange test dates to avoid conflict with school events.	Professors in different courses usually schedule tests without regard to the demands of other courses or outside activities.
Teachers frequently conduct review sessions, pointing out the most important concepts.	Professors rarely offer review sessions, and when they do, they expect you to be an active participant, one who comes prepared with questions.
Guiding principle: Mastery is usually seen as the ability to reproduce what you were taught in the form in which it was presented to you, or to solve the kinds of problems you were shown how to solve.	**Guiding principle:** Mastery is often seen as the ability to apply what you've learned to new situations or to solve new kinds of problems.

How is college different from high school?

GRADES IN HIGH SCHOOL	GRADES IN COLLEGE
Grades are given for most assigned work.	Grades may not be provided for all assigned work.
Consistently good homework grades may raise your overall grade when test grades are low.	Grades on tests and major papers usually provide most of the course grade.
Extra credit projects are often available to help you raise your grade.	Grades on tests and major papers usually provide most of the course grade.
Initial test grades, especially when they are low, may not have an adverse effect on your final grade.	Watch out for your first tests. These are usually "wake-up calls" to let you know what is expected--but they also may account for a substantial part of your course grade. You may be shocked when you get your grades.
You may graduate as long as you have passed all required courses with a grade of D or higher.	You may graduate only if your average in classes meets the departmental standard--typically a 2.0 or C.
Guiding principle: Effort counts. Courses are usually structured to reward a "good-faith effort.	**Guiding principle:** Results count. Though "good-faith effort" is important in regard to the professor's willingness to help you achieve good results, it will not substitute for results in the grading process.

Used with permission from the Altshuler Learning Enhancement Center at Southern Methodist University http://smu.edu/alec/tranisition.asp

Terms for English 1101, 1102, and 1103

Students in English 1101 and 1102/1103 should become familiar with the following terms.

Terms for English 1101

abstract language
adjectives
adverbs
affordances
agreement
antecedent
appositive
audience
audience awareness

claim
clause
coherence
concrete language
conjunctions
connotation
counterargument

deductive reasoning
denotation
diction
documentation
drafting

editing
emphasis
ethos
evidence

fallacy
figurative language
freewriting

generalization

inductive reasoning

jargon

logos

modifier

nouns

opinion

paragraph development
parallelism
paraphrase
pathos
phrase
plagiarism
predicate
prepositions
presentation and document design
pronouns
punctuation

quotations

revising

specific language
subject
summary
support

thesis statement
tone
topic sentence
transition

unity
verbs

Terms for English 1102/1103

alliteration
allegory
analysis
assonance

characters
climax
connotations

denotations
diction
dramatic monologue

ethos

figures of speech
first person

genre

imagery

metaphor

narrative

omniscient author

persona
plot
point of view
protagonist

realism
rhyme
rhythm

schemes
setting
simile
speaker
stage directions
style
symbol and symbolism
syntax

tone

unreliable narrator

voice

From the Director,

Most, although certainly not all, students who take First-year Composition are experiencing their first year at the University of Georgia. This is an exciting, and yet challenging time, as you adjust to the new environment, become acquainted with academic expectations and customs, and learn to manage your time. The FYC Program and *FYC Guide* are designed to support your transition into the university and its academic community, conveying the Program's expectations for you as a student and writer and offering support for studying, thinking, and writing about academic topics. FYC aims to prepare you not only for later academic experiences but also for the world beyond the university, honing the verbal skills and collaborative mindset that employers regularly cite as being important in the workplace.

Dr. Christy Desmet - Director of FYC

Whether or not you are new to UGA, we hope that in First-year Composition you will enjoy the experience of a small class in which you learn to work closely with your instructor and fellow students. Most of all, the faculty and administration of the UGA First-year Composition Program hope that you will enjoy the process of becoming a writer, which can sustain you through your life-long career as a learner.

Robby Nadler - Assistant Director of FYC Writing Center
Dr. Lisa Bolding - Assistant Director of FYC Emma Support (center, standing)
Dr. Deborah Miller - Associate Director of FYC (right)
Jane Barroso - Administrative Assistant II (seated)